T0272459

PHENOMENON

PHENOMENON

THE INCREDIBLE CAREER OF
BRAZIL'S
RONALDO

DANIEL WILLIAMSON

First published by Pitch Publishing, 2023

Pitch Publishing
9 Donnington Park,
85 Birdham Road,
Chichester,
West Sussex,
PO20 7AJ
www.pitchpublishing.co.uk
info@pitchpublishing.co.uk

ISBN 978 1 80150 492 8

Typesetting and origination by Pitch Publishing

Printed and bound in India by Thomson Press India Ltd.

Contents

To my phenomenal girls: Greta, Frieda, and Lottie.

Also by Daniel Williamson

Blue & Gold Passion: A History of Boca Juniors
When Two Worlds Collide: The Intercontinental Cup
Years

Acknowledgements

THANKS TO Pitch Publishing, and Duncan Olner for another incredible cover design.

I have massive gratitude for all the interviewees who gave up their time out of nothing but a desire to help, and a passion to talk football. So, thanks to:

Scotland manager Craig Brown who explained in detail his plan to stop Ronaldo at the 1998 World Cup, and the sage advice he received from Bobby Robson. The Tartan Army lost, but Ronaldo failed to score.

Norwegian defender Henning Berg who recalled playing against Ronaldo three times – in an international friendly, in the World Cup group stage, and for Manchester United against Inter in the 1998/99 Champions League. He was proud to be unbeaten in those games but rates the Brazilian highly.

Björn van der Doelen, Ronaldo's team-mate at PSV Eindhoven for two years between 1994 and 1996. The Dutch midfielder, a similar age to Ronaldo, recounts some funny anecdotes and gives insight into a teenage player moving from Brazil to Europe for the first time.

Craig Buglass and Peter Hudson, two incredibly talented designers from the north of England who passionately recalled their role in helping Nike become the number one brand in football, thanks in no small part to the iconic kits and boots they created.

Chris Terry, who worked for Sky Sports as a reporter covering the 1998 World Cup in France, with a specific focus on Brazil. Thanks to his son Joe Terry for facilitating the conversation.

Real Madrid fan and Brazil-based journalist Eduardo Álvarez recalled Ronaldo's four and a half years at the club. The third *galáctico* produced his best club football in years and is loved at the Bernabéu.

Richard Hall, who works for Inter on their English-language coverage and founded the excellent Gentleman Ultra site. He spoke brilliantly about Ronaldo's Jekyll-and-Hyde five years at the San Siro.

Fernando Duarte, Brazilian author and journalist, spoke to me about the national team's failure at the 2006 World Cup.

Brazilian broadcasters Celzo Unzelte and Roberto Lioi discussed with me Ronaldo's return to his homeland for his Corinthians swansong between 2009 and 2011.

Ciaran Crilly and Frans Claes, who have been season ticket holders at Inter and PSV respectively for almost as long as I've been alive, got to see a youthful Ronaldo in the flesh at his terrifying best.

Thiago Vancellote, the director of commerce and marketing of São Cristóvão FC between February 2019 and November 2021, talked about the legacy of the player at his first 11-a-side club after he transitioned from futsal.

Emmet Gates, who covers Italian football for *Forbes* and has appeared in *The Guardian*, spoke to me about Ronaldo's time with Milan, his final club in European football.

Thanks to Matt Evans for his constant support and reassurance throughout the process.

Thank you to Ryan Baldi.

Thanks to my friend in Rio de Janeiro, Téo Benjamin, for the enjoyable and informal chat about his opinion and memories of Ronaldo.

Thanks to the following people for their advice, support, and for sharing contacts: Alexandre Giesbrecht, Bruno Freitas, Paul Groenendijk, and Emanuel Roşu.

Thanks to the talented journalists whose invaluable work I used as secondary sources to augment my research. They can all be found in the bibliography at the back of the book, and are credited throughout the chapters where possible.

Thanks to my proofreaders: Christopher Hylland, Danny Harvey, Gavin Haverty, Jon McNicoll, Peter Fleming, Niall Owens, Tom Simmonds, Nigel Appleton, Mariano Abrach, Ruairi Criscuolo, and Kiran Nandra.

Finally, thanks to every single person who has bought the book. This was a real labour of love – well, watching endless YouTube videos of Ronaldo wasn't the hard part of the process – but to know people are reading, and hopefully enjoying, it makes the whole process worthwhile.

Introduction

THE MORNING of Sunday, 12 July 1998. Paris. The calm before the storm. The World Cup Final was scheduled for later that evening. It was to be the coronation of world football's young king. The Brazilian with the infectious, buck-toothed smile had almost come out of the womb scoring goals and hadn't stopped. Since making his professional debut he'd ripped the back of the net countless times for Cruzeiro in his homeland, before traversing the Atlantic to do the same in Europe, first with PSV Eindhoven in the Netherlands then Barcelona in Spain.

And then Inter, in Serie A, in the toughest league in the world at the time. The place where many a brilliant forward had tried and failed to do what Ronaldo did in his first season. A haven for defenders, a place with more clean sheets than the local launderette. Not even the Italian league could contain Ronaldo, and it was during this time the press dubbed him *Il Fenónemo*, a nickname which doesn't need translating. The two-time FIFA World Player of the Year, and the incumbent Ballon d'Or holder, was on top of the world. It was going to be *his* final.

As 9pm Central European Time approached, rumours began spreading across the French capital like wildfire. Then, in the days before the internet, before news reached the four

13

corners of the world in a matter of milliseconds, the rest of us were introduced to the incredible plot via the biggest game of Chinese whispers ever played. Everyone had a theory, an opinion. Everyone knew the answer. Yet nobody knew anything at the same time. Only those closest to Ronaldo had the faintest idea of what had happened that afternoon, and even now, their stories are contradictory.

Ronaldo emerged on to the pitch in Saint-Denis a shell of the formidable force that had eviscerated everything in his path prior to that evening. Football's answer to the Terminator appeared to have been terminated. For 90 minutes, he cut a ghost-like figure as Zinedine Zidane and *Les Bleus* won comfortably to lift the famous trophy on home turf. To continue with the 1980s movie analogies, the World Cup in 1998 was the first time we saw Ronaldo as a human. Like in *Rocky IV,* when the Italian Stallion cuts imposing Soviet destroyer Ivan Drago with a vicious punch, and back in the corner his trainer, Duke, shouts, 'You see? He's not a machine! He's a man!'

* * *

It's hard to pinpoint the exact moment I became aware of Ronaldo. Although the 1994 World Cup, held in the United States, was the first one I fully consumed in its entirety, despite the unsociable kick-off times, it's likely that I knew nothing then of a scrawny 17-year-old whose backside remained firmly planted to Brazil's bench for the duration of the tournament, while the diminutive duo of Bebeto and Romário fired the *Seleção* to glory. It may have been Channel 4's *Trans World Sport*, or *Eurogoals* on Eurosport when he played for PSV. Many a Tuesday morning in school was spent bleary-eyed having stayed up past my bedtime watching goals fly in across obscure leagues on the continent. Ronaldo will have come to the attention of an English crowd in 1995 when scoring at Wembley for Brazil in a 3-1 win over the Three Lions in the Umbro Cup, a friendly tournament that acted as a dress rehearsal for the 1996 European Championship.

By the time he signed for Barcelona in 1996, I was a fully paid-up member of the Ronaldo fan club. I bought the stunning home shirt, made by Kappa, a long-sleeved version. The blue and red colours combine majestically. I was able to watch him perform for Barça, as La Liga was shown by Sky Sports and we had a dodgy, chipped cable box. I hope the statute of limitations on that admission has expired and I won't get a knock on the door from the piracy police.

He signed for Inter in 1997, joining the best league in the world at the time, one that luckily was shown by Channel 4 in the form of a live Sunday afternoon match, as well as the iconic Saturday morning highlights show, *Gazzetta Football Italia*. Everyone remembers James Richardson sipping a coffee in some idyllic town square while reading the headlines from the pink newspaper. I bought the black and blue home shirt, manufactured by Umbro. Any time we played 'Wembley Singles/Doubles', or I was kicking the ball in the garden much to the annoyance of the neighbours, I would mimic his arms-out celebration after scoring. For someone who had grown up idolising Manchester United players, and to a lesser extent England stars, Ronaldo was perhaps the first 'other' player I hero-worshipped.

When it came to the 1998 World Cup Final in Paris I, like billions of others tuning in across the globe, couldn't wait to watch him perform on the biggest stage. I was truly devastated to hear the news that he was to miss out, shocked and confused when it transpired he was back in the XI and hurt when he failed to fulfil his potential with the eyes of the world upon him.

* * *

Ronaldo's redemption story is worthy of a Hollywood movie. The four years after that fateful night in Paris would have destroyed a lesser man, with more than one career-threatening injury followed by demoralising, failed comeback attempts. By the time the 2002 World Cup in Japan and South Korea came around, few would have predicted what happened next. With two goals in the final against Germany in Yokohama, Ronaldo exorcised the demons of Paris, the man of the match as his country became the first – and to this day, only – to win the World Cup five times. A new, different Ronaldo he may have been, but he was still the best striker on the planet. His purchase by Real Madrid – deep into their famous *galácticos* project – following the tournament was vindication that he was back on the throne.

Ronaldo is one of the most-loved strikers modern football has seen and will feature in most people's lists of the greatest number nine to lace up a pair of ultra-lightweight boots. Videos of his feats, some of it now admittedly grainy and far from HD, regularly do the rounds on social media, shared widely by many far too young to have seen him in the flesh. His story, talent, and smile mean he transcends generations.

The two World Cups that are so pivotal to his story, plus everything before, after, and in between, are covered in these pages. From his humble roots to his meteoric rise; from his fall, second rise, retirement, and conversion to a successful businessman. This is the story of the Phenomenon.

Chapter 1

Dadado, the Boy With Two Birthdays

IT WAS at the São Francisco Xavier hospital, on 18 September 1976, that Sônia gave birth to her third child. Weighing 3.3kg, the boy was named after the man who delivered him: Dr Ronaldo Valente. Sônia had superstitiously not planned a name, believing it to be a bad omen, and chose the new arrival's moniker rather spontaneously.

Like many of football's greats, Ronaldo was born into humble surroundings. They had few luxuries, but he wasn't raised in abject poverty. Bento Ribeiro is a working-class neighbourhood in Rio de Janeiro's North Zone, where he lived with his older siblings, sister Ione and brother Nelinho, at the family home on Rua General César Obino.

Sônia, then 25, worked hard to provide for her children, working long hours in menial jobs for modest pay. She took pride in her home and her young family. The fiercely independent woman was determined not to have to rely on her husband, Nélio, a loveable but wayward rogue whom she had originally met when working for the state telecommunications company.

Ronaldo's father spent days celebrating the new arrival, neglecting to register the birth immediately. The story goes that to avoid a fine, he lied, stating that the baby had been born on 22 September. The boy's official name was listed as Ronaldo Luís Nazário de Lima.

The young Ronaldo slept with his parents, as he feared the dark. He occasionally wet the bed and used to sleepwalk. Later, he moved on to a sofa bed in the living room of the one-bedroom house. Having trouble pronouncing his name, he was affectionately nicknamed *Dadado*.

It was at the age of four that his lifelong obsession with football began when he received a lightweight plastic ball for Christmas. During daylight hours, Ronaldo couldn't be separated from his favourite new toy; kicking it around the dusty streets became more of a lifestyle and an identity than a hobby. He honed his craft on the bumpy, unforgiving, unpredictable surfaces. When he wasn't playing, he was dreaming about a future in which he could forge a career out of the game. His mother did well to shield him from the bad things happening in the neighbourhood.

In the summer of 1982, Ronaldo experienced the event that is crystallised in the minds of most football obsessives: their first World Cup. As is the tradition in Brazil, the kerb stones of Bento Ribeiro were painted in bright blue, green and yellow. Murals of heroes and the Brazilian flag were daubed on to the neighbourhood walls. Many in the community watched the games at Mr Renato's house, and the kids were treated to soft drinks and French fries. Ronaldo cried as Italy dumped the *Seleção* out of the tournament.

He attended the Colégio Nossa Senhora de Aparecida but, like many footballers, his passion lay beyond the four walls of the classroom. Much to his mum's annoyance he preferred to spend time with a ball rather than with his head buried in books. 'I could not accept the fact that my son thought only of playing soccer,' she told Rio newspaper *O Globo* in a 1997 interview. 'What kind of future would he have? I always found him on the street playing ball with friends when he should have been in school. I know, I lost my battle.'

When he was slightly older, Ronaldo and his friends jumped the train at the weekends, heading south to play informal matches and foot-volley on Rio's famous golden beaches. As well as street football, playing on sand required a different skill set, providing a well-rounded education to the future footballer.

His first foray into organised sport came via futsal, a modified form of football particularly popular in South America and southern Europe. It uses a smaller, heavier ball and therefore tends to develop footballers with excellent close control. Unlike indoor football in the United Kingdom, where the pitches are enclosed by walls that can be used to bounce the ball off, there are boundaries in futsal, and the ball has to be controlled within the lines.

In 1986 Brazil were eliminated from the Mexico World Cup by France, following a penalty shoot-out. Around this time, the nine-year-old Ronaldo joined Valqueire, a tennis and sports club founded in 1963, one that now proudly boasts to have started his career. For his family, the bonus was that they were able to use the leisure club facilities for free. His first position was goalkeeper until one game where he played outfield, scoring four in a 5-4 victory over league leaders Vasco. He never donned the gloves again.

When Ronaldo was 11, his parents, perhaps unsurprisingly, split. Their personalities and dedication to the family home were at the opposite ends of the spectrum, and Nélio was spending more of his time and money in neighbourhood drinking establishments. With a single parent running the household, the financial situation became much tighter for the family.

In 1988, Fernando 'Gordo' dos Santos Carvalho recruited the youngster to join him at the more established Social Ramos club. To persuade his sceptical mother, Gordo promised to pick Ronaldo up and drop him off at home afterwards and reassured her that the club would provide boots and kit.

Even at such a young age, Ronaldo was showing traits that would stand him in good stead throughout his professional career. In Jorge Caldeira's book *Ronaldo: Gloria e Drama no Futebol Globalizado*, Alirio Carvalho – one of Ronaldo's coaches at Social Ramos – said, 'What was special about him was his attitude. It was as if he had come from the moon. Nothing disturbed him, nothing overawed him, nothing threw him off his game.' After a record 166 goals in his first season, including 11 in one match, a bigger stage was required.

When he was 13, a dream trial with the club he supported, Flamengo, materialised. The team of his idol, Zico, and Brazil's most popular club, the *Rubro-Negro* were based on the other side of the city, in Gávea. For Ronaldo, it was a long trip that required him to travel alone, on two buses. Alongside 400 others, Ronaldo was part of the *peneira* (sifter), where the hopefuls are observed in a series of small-sided games. It's hardly an exact science, and there are numerous examples of players slipping through the net only to go on to have excellent professional careers. Ronaldo, however, did enough to be asked to return the following day. He asked for support with the 30 centavos bus fare, but his request fell on unsympathetic, deaf ears. To cap off a miserable day, he was mugged on the way home, losing his watch.

In 1990, the year Brazil's World Cup drought stretched to two decades in Italy, Ronaldo signed for his first 11-a-side team. One that played on grass. The version of the game in which he would make his name and fortune. Along with his friend, Alexandre Calango, the teenager joined São Cristóvão, a club founded in 1898 and based in the neighbourhood of the same name. São Cristóvão peaked in the 1920s, but by the decade of Ronaldo's birth was in steady decline. An expressway was built next to the ground which effectively hid it from view. On the other end, it's wedged in by a factory which makes spectacle lenses. Just two kilometres away stands the iconic Maracanã Stadium, the cathedral of Brazilian football where Ronaldo had watched his first professional match – Flamengo versus Vasco da Gama – with his father. Located in the north of the city, less than 20km from Ronaldo's home, proved a much more favourable distance for the promising youngster to travel. Unlike Flamengo, São Cristóvão were also happy to help out with transportation.

It was the club's general director, Ary Ferreiras de Sá, who brought the player to the Cadets, having struck a deal with his counterpart at Social Ramos to let some of their youngsters give the full-sized version of the game a go. The gangly forward quickly rose through São Cristóvão's youth ranks, scoring five in a friendly tournament soon after his arrival, and bagging a hat-trick on his under-15 debut in a 5-2 win over Tomazinho in August 1990. His stock rose rapidly and before long he was playing for the under-20s.

São Cristóvão coach Alfredo Sampaio described the youngster to Joshua Law, writing for Planet Football, in 2021, 'If there was a time that he didn't play as well, it was because of him, never because of the pressure of the game. He was never shaken by the occasion. He was like Garrincha. He didn't care who he was playing against, he wanted to play. He trusted himself, and he was having fun.'

At this point, Ronaldo, as well as his inability to be flustered, was also described as a lazy trainer – an accusation that would stay with him for most of his career – and despite his goals he was not particularly tactically aware. He was still trying to shake off some of the habits formed in futsal. He had a pleasant, if not cheeky, demeanour as a young man although he was at times shy and a little socially awkward. At São Cristóvão he was nicknamed 'Monica', after a buck-toothed character from a popular comic book turned cartoon.

Finding the back of the net became a habit and in January 1993 Ronaldo was promoted to the first team, then plying its trade in the top division of Rio's state league system. International recognition was also forthcoming and he was called up for the South American U-17 Championship, which took place in February in Colombia. Brazil won all four games in the first phase. However, in the final stage they failed to win, missing out on a place in the FIFA U-17 World Cup in Japan. The competition was a disaster for Brazil, but on a personal note Ronaldo's eight goals added to his burgeoning stock. At club level he'd scored 44 for São Cristóvão, all from open play. Soon, with the help of two men he'd met the year before, Ronaldo would make the transition from an amateur footballer to a fully fledged professional, the next step on his exciting journey.

Chapter 2

Beautiful Horizon

IN A practice that was common in Brazil, former bankers turned football agents Reinaldo Pitta and Alexandre Martins bought Ronaldo's contract from São Cristóvão for US$7,500. Alfredo Sampaio had recommended the player to the pair, and they were sufficiently impressed when they watched him score five in a 9-1 win for the Cadets. 'We saw right away that he could be something different than most other players,' Pitta said.

They signed Ronaldo to an unbreakable ten-year deal which covered transfer fees and image rights. Put simply, if the talented footballer was to make any money going forward, a chunk of it would fall into his new agents' pockets. The pair would have a major influence over his career during the next two decades and the initial investment would prove to be one of the shrewdest in the sport's history. Not everyone was impressed, however. The deal was signed not by Ronaldo, as he was too young, but his father, on 7 June 1992. Jorge Caldeira, the author of a Ronaldo biography, said the agreement was like some of the servitude deals from the era of slavery.

As Ronaldo continued to plunder goals for São Cristóvão and later Brazil's youth teams, many of the country's biggest clubs started to circle. Advances by Botafogo and São Paulo were rebuffed and, ultimately, Cruzeiro – based in Belo Horizonte – won the battle for his signature. Ronaldo was valued at US$50,000.

Belo Horizonte, which translates as 'Beautiful Horizon', is the capital of Minas Gerais state and was Brazil's first planned city. Approximately 400km from Rio, it might as well have been on another planet to the 16-year-old. Founded in 1921, the *Celeste* won their first Copa Libertadores title in the year of Ronaldo's birth, that triumph coming a decade after they won the national Série A. When it came to state championships, the club was highly decorated.

Ronaldo represented the under-20 side, bagging four goals on his debut, and took to each new challenge like a duck to water. Less than three months after his arrival, on 25 May 1993, the skinny teenager was given his first-team debut by the head coach in a state championship match against Caldense. Pinheiro asked youth team coach Baiano for a few youngsters to pad out the squad, resting key stars ahead of the Copa do Brasil semi-final second leg against Vasco da Gama. Cruzeiro beat Caldense 1-0 and although Ronaldo – a few months shy of his 17th birthday – had a quiet game, in front of less than 2,500 paying spectators, he was on the next rung of the ladder.

Ronaldo continued to score goals for the youth team and in the summer of 1993 headed to the United States to represent Brazil's under-17s in a tournament intended to be a test event for the World Cup of the following year. Then, Cruzeiro's new coach, Carlos Alberto Silva, took the prodigious youngster with the first team on a tour to Portugal, where they played friendlies against local giants Benfica and Porto, as well as Belenenses and Uruguayan outfit Peñarol. Appearing in all four games, Ronaldo scored two goals, impressing everyone who caught a glimpse of his burgeoning talent. The Belenenses goalkeeper had bestowed upon him the honour of conceding Ronaldo's first senior goal. Many of his peers would soon suffer the same fate. The second strike came against Peñarol, by all accounts a stunning individual goal that – unfortunately – no footage exists of.

Just five months into his stay in Belo Horizonte, Porto were moved enough to offer US$500,000 although Cruzeiro's president Cesar Masci wanted US$750,000 and Ronaldo stayed put. There would be no return to the youth team this time. When it came to senior football, Ronaldo had well and truly arrived.

In the Campeonato Brasileiro, which ran from September to December 1993, Cruzeiro missed out on qualification for the next round by two points. Ronaldo scored in matches against Bahia, São Paulo, and Bragantino, as well as netting home and away versus Botafogo. He even scored in a home defeat to the reigning national champions, his beloved Flamengo.

On 7 November he scored a stunning five goals at the Mineirão against Bahia. Their goalkeeper, Rodolfo Rodríguez, then 37, had a torrid afternoon. He conceded a penalty which was converted by Ronaldo, who then set up the second for Careca. Three more followed. With the final whistle closing in, a frustrated and shell-shocked Rodríguez saved a shot and sat on his knees with the ball in his hands. Looking to the sky and putting his head in his hands almost in disbelief at the way the afternoon was unfolding, he wasn't to know it was about to get worse.

Showing the impudence of youth, and the predatory instincts that make a great forward, Ronaldo was lurking behind the experienced goalkeeper, and as soon as Rodríguez released it to stand up, he nipped in and rolled the ball into the net to make it 6-0. Rodríguez retired the following year as Uruguay's most capped player, with 78 appearances, and it wouldn't be surprising if that day's events played a part in his decision to hang up the gloves. It would be easy for him to think it was evidence of his dulling senses, yet many more goalkeepers would be made to look foolish in the ensuing years. 'The only thing he didn't do that day was make it rain in the Mineirão,' said Careca in a 2021 interview with Joshua Law for Planet Football. 'That's when he started to grab the attention of the world. Playing with Ronaldo was easy because his quality was so far above average. He played and made all the other players, all his colleagues, play and grow and give a better account of themselves. He made the game easier and did something that today is rare, he was a forward who decided games by himself. It came easily to Ronaldo.'

The game was widely discussed on television; Ronaldo's stock was rising. Dida, who went on to keep goal for Brazil and Milan, was also a colleague at Cruzeiro. The stopper said Ronaldo was the club's biggest star since Tostão, a legend of Brazil's 1970 World Cup-winning team. Dida was also Ronaldo's unofficial chauffeur. The club president had bought the young forward a car but as he didn't have a driving licence, Dida did the honours. He remarked that the downside of car sharing with Ronaldo was the sheer time it took to escape the training ground, autograph hunters swarming the car daily.

A week later, Ronaldo's final goal of the tournament came in a 4-1 win over Internacional. In the Supercopa Libertadores, which took place across October and November 1993 and featured past winners of the Copa Libertadores, Ronaldo was in fine form against established continental names. In the first round, he scored five over two legs as Chilean outfit Colo-Colo, South

American champions just two years earlier, were brushed aside 9-4 on aggregate. Although Cruzeiro's run ended in the quarter-final, Ronaldo still managed three goals in two games against Nacional of Uruguay, who progressed to the final four on penalties. Even though the semis and final were still to come, Ronaldo had done enough to finish as the competition's highest scorer.

Ronaldo also enhanced his reputation in the 1994 Copa Libertadores. Cruzeiro – qualifying as Copa do Brasil holders – were drawn in a tough group with Boca Juniors, Brazilian champions Palmeiras, and eventual winners Vélez Sarsfield. He scored in a 1-1 draw at home to Vélez and then a week later Cruzeiro travelled to La Bombonera. In front of a typically boisterous crowd – which included Diego Maradona in his executive box – Ronaldo's apprenticeship showed him how tough he'd have to be to make it at the highest level. He was kicked from pillar to post but it wasn't for nothing – following one of many fouls on Ronaldo, Paulo Roberto slammed home the resulting free kick and Cruzeiro went on to win 2-1.

Going into the last matchday, at home to Boca, Cruzeiro needed a win to guarantee progress to the knockout phase. It would be a night when Ronaldo would exact his revenge, with skill, not violence. The precocious youngster set the tone with a first-minute nutmeg on Carlos Moya. Boca took the lead, following a mistake by Dida, but Ronaldo assisted Luis Fernando to bring the sides level. With 15 minutes to go, Ronaldo took centre stage. Finding a pocket of space in the centre circle, he took the ball on the half turn and ran at the tiring defence. He burst through a trio of Boca defenders then, when faced with Carlos Navarro Montoya, he took the ball around the goalkeeper and slid it into the empty net. 'I got the ball in midfield, and when I turned a few players came towards me, but I dribbled around them all,' he told the club's in-house magazine. 'When I got into the area, I took it around the goalkeeper Navarro Montoya and just touched it into the net. A defender tried to stop it by sliding in, but he ended up in the goal as well. It was a *golaço*, unforgettable.'

Cruzeiro limped out of the Copa Libertadores after an uninspiring last-16 defeat at the hands of Unión Española. The following month they wrapped up the Minas Gerais state championship, obliterating the competition in the process. After 22 matches, the Foxes were unbeaten, finishing ten points clear in the era of two points for a win. They scored 59, conceding just 15. Ronaldo finished as the competition's top scorer with 22 goals in 18 games, winning his first title as a player in the process.

The highlight of Cruzeiro's state championship triumph for Ronaldo came on 6 March against Atlético Mineiro, in front of 70,000 fans. Under a deluge of torrential rain, Ronaldo scored a hat-trick in a 3-1 derby win. For the Cruzeiro fans, a highlight of the night was when the young forward left Uruguayan centre-back Fernando Kanapkis on his backside not once, but twice. 'He destroyed the game,' Careca told Joshua Law. 'He didn't only destroy the game, but he destroyed Kanapkis. He left Kanapkis sat on the floor. The Cruzeiro fans gave him a three-minute standing ovation.'

Ronaldo's exciting displays for his club side led to senior international recognition before too long. In November 1993, not long after his five-goal haul against Bahia, Carlos Alberto Parreira called him up for the squad to face Germany in a friendly in Cologne. Although he didn't get any minutes, it was a promising sign that he was in the coach's thoughts ahead of the World Cup the following summer. His debut for the Seleção came on 23 March 1994 in a friendly against Brazil's neighbours and arch rivals, Argentina. In front of a bumper crowd in Recife, the 17-year-old watched from the bench as Bebeto scored twice. With ten minutes to go, Ronaldo replaced the scorer for his first taste of senior international football as Brazil won 2-0. Diego Maradona, racing to be fit for the showpiece tournament, watched from the stands.

On 4 May, Brazil hosted Iceland in Florianópolis, just three days after the tragic death of F1 legend Ayrton Senna had devastated the country. At the business end of their season, European clubs refused to release their stars for the match, which paved the way for domestic-based talent such as Ronaldo. He started the match, wearing number seven, netting the first goal in a 3-0 win with a left-footed strike from the edge of the box. Five days later, he was named in the squad for the biggest football tournament on the planet. Under-fire pragmatist Parreira couldn't ignore Ronaldo who had been scoring for fun for Cruzeiro and had now grabbed his first goal for the national team.

Under a blazing July sun in Pasadena's Rose Bowl, Brazil beat Italy on penalties to lift their fourth World Cup, ending an agonising 24-year drought. Although the final – contested by two exhausted teams – failed to live up to the billing, the form of diminutive front pair Bebeto and Romário throughout the tournament ensured Ronaldo's backside stayed firmly glued to the bench for the full duration.

It was also the demands on Parreira to win the tournament which ensured the coach sided with experience throughout. A country that is obsessed with the World Cup, it would have heaped immense pressure on the teenager's shoulders had he been thrust into the limelight too early and on such a big stage. No doubt he will have learned an intangible amount from Bebeto and Romário. Soon, Ronaldo would become a legitimate rival of theirs for a spot in the starting XI.

The lack of minutes didn't dampen the youngster's celebrations, though, pristine in his unused kit, shin pads on under his dazzling white socks just in case he was ever pressed into action. Draped in the Brazil flag, he celebrated with his team-mates and kissed the famous trophy. He swapped shirts with Italy's Pierluigi Casiraghi, the Lazio striker who would become a Serie A contemporary within three years. The inevitable Pelé comparisons came; *O Rei* had played for Brazil at the World Cup in 1958 at the same tender age.

Ronaldo summed up his experience at the World Cup in a 2015 article on the Players' Tribune website, 'Sometimes it felt like I went from one day playing at school and in our backyard, to practising with Bebeto ... playing with that team in that tournament was like going to the Ivy League of football. It was a first-class, front-row education on how to not just play football, but how to *be* a footballer. How to be a World Cup champion ... I didn't play a minute in that tournament, but I watched and absorbed everything that I could. I took notes, collected all this information, knowing that someday I was going to be back ... That summer changed my life and my career.'

After the tournament the youngster, who had been playing for modest São Cristóvão just 18 months earlier, returned to Belo Horizonte, but not for long. Forty-four competitive goals in just over a year following his debut in May 1993 showed that Ronaldo had outgrown Brazilian football. He'd starred at home at a time when most of the Seleção's stars were plying their trade abroad. For Cruzeiro, who struggled in the 1980s, Ronaldo was part of a renaissance which saw the club regain some credibility; three years later they would lift the Copa Libertadores for the first time in 21 years. For Ronaldo, Europe beckoned.

Chapter 3

Path to Superstardom

PSV EINDHOVEN won the European Cup in 1988 and, backed by electronics giant Philips, further strengthened their squad by signing a 22-year-old Romário, who had just starred as Brazil picked up a silver medal at the Seoul Olympics. Over the next five years they then won three league titles as well as the KNVB Cup on two occasions. Having failed to adequately replace Romário, who moved to Barcelona in 1993 to join Johan Cruyff's Dream Team, an experienced but ageing PSV side finished third as Ajax lifted the title. Ahead of the 1994/95 season they needed a new talisman, and Ronaldo fitted the bill perfectly.

The youngster came to the attention of PSV in late 1993, although they didn't follow up on their initial interest as the board worried about his lack of international experience and was unsure whether he'd be able to translate his prolific South American form to Europe. By the time of his transfer, however, his stock had risen considerably and the price of acquiring his services quadrupled. Clubs of the ilk of Porto, Bayern Munich and AC Milan were circling, and PSV's eagerness to pay the $6m swung it for them ahead of more illustrious rivals. It was a costly spot of procrastination, but they got their man. Ronaldo had met with

PSV sporting director Frank Arnesen in California while on World Cup duty.

Romário did his old club a favour, convincing his international colleague to sign on the dotted line at the Philips Stadion, suggesting it was the perfect bridge between South America and one of Europe's leading clubs, as his trajectory had proven. 'Romário told me that PSV is one of the most professional and best-organised clubs in Europe,' said Ronaldo. 'He said it would be best to acclimatise in Europe and to learn about European football.'

PSV was a well-run, friendly club, with a real family vibe. It had also been a solid breeding ground for the likes of Ruud Gullit and Ronald Koeman who had left for AC Milan and Barcelona respectively. Ronaldo joined the Dutch club shortly after the World Cup in the United States had concluded. Cruzeiro, while sad to see the rising star depart, were happy to bank the fee which helped pay off their debts and put them on an even keel. In 1997, with newfound solidity, they won the Copa Libertadores. Pitta and Martins were also delighted, pocketing a healthy commission from the transfer.

Despite his World Cup medal and a bagful of goals in South American football, Ronaldo was still relatively unknown in Europe. 'We had seen some flashes of him scoring goals for his club on Dutch TV because both PSV and Ajax wanted him,' said Frans Claes, who has been a PSV season ticket holder since 1985. Luckily for Ajax, their manager Louis van Gaal placed his faith in his young striker, Patrick Kluivert.

Ronaldo arrived with little fanfare, his unveiling a low-key affair. You can count on one hand the number of journalists who showed up to see him – wearing a long-sleeved replica shirt, blue jeans, and black loafers – performing tricks with the ball on the pitch at the Philips Stadion. To help the teenager settle, PSV provided an interpreter and Ronaldo quickly reached a passable level of Dutch. A house in a quiet suburb was provided, filled with the latest electronic gadgets from Philips. However, a young boy still needs his mother so Sônia relocated to the Netherlands and the pair soon found a larger home. Her presence helped him settle, allowing him to focus on football and flourish on the pitch. In October, Stan Valckx arrived from Sporting. Having spent three years in Lisbon, the Dutch defender was able to converse with Ronaldo in his native Portuguese.

Ronaldo wasn't the only youngster making his name in the first team as manager Aad de Mos looked to renovate the squad and bring down the average age after the previous, disappointing campaign. 'A few national team players were still on holiday following the World Cup in the United States, so young players like me, Bolo Zenden and Tommie van der Leegte made up the numbers in pre-season to see if we could handle the level of the first team,' said Dutch midfielder Björn van der Doelen. 'After that, we were supposed to return to the second team, but we stayed with the first team when the national team players returned. We were 18 years old.'

'It's nothing now, but in those days, it was a lot of money,' said Van der Doelen, recalling his first impression of Ronaldo. 'At one of the first training sessions, Ronaldo was a bit lazy, so De Mos made him shoot at an empty goal over and over again as a punishment. Every shot went over or wide. However, in one of the first games he played he showed he was incredible and within a few months we knew we had one hell of a player.'

Just nine minutes into his competitive debut Ronaldo latched on to a Luc Nilis pass, took a touch then calmly rolled the ball past

Vitesse Arnhem goalkeeper Raimond van der Gouw. Nilis – the Belgian with whom Ronaldo struck up a fruitful partnership – grabbed two goals of his own as PSV ran out 4-2 winners on the opening day of the Eredivisie season. 'Everybody immediately saw his talent,' said Frans Claes, who as well as being an ever-present at the Philips Stadion also collects PSV-related memorabilia. It took Ronaldo even less time to get on the scoresheet on his home debut against Go Ahead Eagles, his first of two goals coming after just one minute. Nilis made it four before the visitors grabbed a consolation. It was an emphatic start to the domestic league campaign.

On 13 September 1994, PSV travelled to Germany to take on Bayer Leverkusen in the first round, first leg of the UEFA Cup. If his name wasn't ringing out across Europe before, it certainly was after the teenager bagged a hat-trick. Rudi Völler, who was winding down his career with Bayer before retiring, didn't feature as he was commentating on German television. He said, 'Never in my life have I seen an 18-year-old play in this way.' If it somehow makes it more impressive, Völler was mistaken; he was still only 17. Just. The fact that Ronaldo's side exited the competition after a goalless draw in the second leg was a footnote in the grand scheme of his meteoric rise.

'We realised how extraordinary he was against Bayer Leverkusen,' said Frans Claes. 'Following the match, a German sports programme invited him to go on the show. The German audience also saw that he was extraordinary.' Even the great Franz Beckenbauer was effusive with praise in the German press. 'You could already see he was special during training, but against Leverkusen the whole world could see how incredibly good he was,' said Van der Doelen, an unused substitute that night in the Ulrich-Haberland-Stadion (now the BayArena).

After another convincing win in the league, Ronaldo then scored an equaliser against Sparta Rotterdam to rescue a point on the road. Oddly, the squad travelled to Mexico City to face Club América in a friendly to mark the South American country's capital club's 78th anniversary, a game arranged as part of the deal that took PSV's Zambian forward Kalusha Bwalya to Mexico. The fixture ended 3-1 to Bwalya's new employers, but the trip helped Ronaldo bond further with his team-mates. 'He was still a kid, but he was a good guy, and still a little childish; he liked to fool around a little bit,' began Van der Doelen, laughing as he recalls happy memories. 'We played in the Azteca Stadium, and he was standing in the dressing room completely naked with only his boots on, playing with the ball. That's one of the things I remember. He was well-liked. He was always happy.'

Back in the Netherlands, a late penalty from Ronaldo sealed a 3-1 win at home to Heerenveen. PSV were unbeaten after six games, averaging three goals per 90 minutes in the league. Then, however, the wheels came off in late October. Three league defeats in nine days – the only consolation being a 5-0 win over Groningen, in which Ronaldo scored – cost De Mos his job. The first of those reverses was an unforgivable 4-1 drubbing by Ajax in front of the Eindhoven crowd. Kees Rijvers – who managed the club with great distinction in the 1970s, winning three league titles, two KNVB Cups, and the UEFA Cup – assumed caretaker control, leading PSV to a 2-1 win in Utrecht, with Ronaldo and Nilis finding the target. Ronaldo bagged a brace in a 4-0 win over MVV then scored two more as free-scoring PSV thumped Feyenoord 4-1 at the Philips Stadion.

After the winter break, PSV's third coach of the season was in place. Dick Advocaat, who had just led the *Oranje* to the quarter-final of the 1994 World Cup, took the reins for the first game back, away to Ajax on 22 January. It was an inauspicious start; PSV lost 1-0 to a Kluivert penalty. However, the points – and Ronaldo's goals – flowed freely after that. He scored twice in a 5-0 win at home to Roda JC, one in a 2-0 win over FC Dordrecht, one in a 3-2 win at home to Vitesse Arnhem, then a brace in a comfortable 4-0 victory at home to Sparta Rotterdam.

A draw at Go Ahead Eagles was followed by a 3-0 home win – and a Ronaldo double – at home to MEC, and after maximum points from the next two games he was back on the scoresheet in a 3-2 win over Willem II. PSV then lost by the same score away to Groningen, Ronaldo's 70th-minute goal proving to be just a consolation. A week later Ronaldo got three in a home thrashing of Utrecht, then the winner in a 3-2 win at MVV. He scored in wins over Twente and RKC Waalwijk, as well as in a 3-2 defeat at De Kuip. On the last day of the league season he bagged a brace in a 4-2 home defeat at the hands of NAC Breda.

PSV finished third, once again qualifying for the UEFA Cup, although they were 14 points off the eventual champions, Ajax, who also lifted the European Cup. The Amsterdam giants went 34 games without losing in the Eredivisie, with a goal difference double that of PSV's. Despite Ronaldo's brilliance, and goals, there was a lot of ground to make up. Although his team failed to lift silverware, Ronaldo's first campaign in Europe was an undoubted success on a personal level. He'd proven beyond doubt that he could make the transition, despite his continual aversion to training and the fact he was the only PSV player to regularly avoid the weights room. The league's top scorer bagged 35 in 36 games, even topping Romário's first-season return at the Philips Stadion, just as the precocious, cheeky youngster had promised.

The football was quicker than South America, but much less physically intimidating, and Ronaldo had settled in superbly.

* * *

Ronaldo was not yet 19, but the summer of 1995 would put his powerful yet still developing frame under intense pressure. There is often talk of modern footballers having a heavy workload and while that may be true, it's nothing new or groundbreaking. The forward participated in two international competitions when most of his colleagues were recuperating after a long, hard season. Six days after the last Eredivisie game, the Umbro Cup kicked off. Featuring England, Brazil, Japan and Sweden, the tournament – held over eight days across five English cities – was a dress rehearsal for Euro '96.

England opened proceedings with a win over Japan at Wembley, and the following day Edmundo's goal separated Brazil and Sweden at Elland Road. In the next round of fixtures, Brazil brushed the Japanese aside, 3-0 at Goodison Park; England and Sweden shared six goals at the home of Leeds United. Although the format of the competition was a round-robin group, the organisers got their wish of a de facto final between England and Brazil on the last matchday. With just two points separating the teams going into the Wembley clash, the ball lay in Brazil's court. England had to win.

A stunning strike from Graeme Le Saux gave Terry Venables's England a half-time lead which they held until ten minutes into the second half when Juninho – who went on to join Middlesbrough in the Premier League just a few months later – equalised with an expertly placed free kick. The diminutive Juninho turned architect for Brazil's second seven minutes later, sliding a perfectly placed pass in between England's experimental centre-half pairing of John Scales and Colin Cooper. Ronaldo, whose movement was excellent in anticipation of the pass, latched on to the ball, his first touch taking him to the side of Tim Flowers, engineering the space which allowed him to roll the ball into the empty net.

It was his second Brazil goal and even Pelé applauded from the grand old stands of Wembley. Ronaldo was replaced a minute before Edmundo made it 3-1 to hand the trophy to the men in yellow. For the popular Venables, it was the only defeat in open play he would suffer while manager of England.

The next stop for the well-travelled teenager was Uruguay for the Copa América. Across 18 days, all ten CONMEBOL nations – plus guests Mexico and the United States – battled for the prestigious trophy. Mário Zagallo's men reached the final, losing to the hosts on penalties. Ronaldo, wearing number 20, didn't appear for a single minute. Like the World Cup the previous summer, it was very much a watching brief but valuable experience, nonetheless.

* * *

PSV started the 1995/96 season like a freight train, losing just one of the first 15 league games. Ronaldo's first goals came in matchday three when he bagged a brace in an emphatic 5-1 home win over Heerenveen. In the UEFA Cup first round first leg PSV surprisingly fell behind to Finnish outfit MyPa, courtesy of a stunning volley by Sami Mahlio. Ronaldo grabbed an away goal after 50 minutes but it wouldn't be needed in the second leg as PSV trounced the minnows 7-1 in Eindhoven, the Brazilian helping himself to four. It was in this tie that he performed a superb double nutmeg, putting the ball through two opponents' legs with two consecutive touches. It was a shame that the resulting shot was dragged just wide of the far post, but it was inventive and bold forward play.

He scored another two in a 3-0 win over Twente, the opener in a 5-0 win at Volendam, and one at home to Feyenoord who were sent back to Rotterdam after a 3-0 defeat. In Salvador, Brazil, he bagged a double for the national team in a home friendly win over Uruguay. Inter supremo Massimo Moratti was reportedly in the crowd, keeping tabs on one of the hottest prospects in European football.

After missing a handful of club games in October due to a combination of international duty and knee complaints, Ronaldo scored in a 1-1 draw away to Ajax on 5 November. Two goals in an 8-0 demolition of De Graafschap followed, then two more in a 5-0 rout of NEC Nijmegen. PSV were progressing well in the UEFA Cup, moving into the last eight after a 2-1 aggregate win over Werder Bremen. Ronaldo started the ball rolling with a penalty in the first leg. Going into the winter break, PSV had lost just twice in the first 18 league games.

A 2-1 defeat to Sparta Rotterdam in early December proved to be the last football Ronaldo played for over four months, the first cracks in the previously infallible young frame beginning to show. And little did anyone know that his 59th-minute strike against NEC Nijmegen would be his last goal for the club. Just after Christmas 1996 he was diagnosed with Osgood-Schlatter disease, a relatively rare condition found most often in young athletes who are growing at the same time they are placing extreme strain on their developing bodies. The main symptom is pain and swelling just below the knee, where the patellar tendon connects with the shin bone.

In his native Rio, after an operation, Ronaldo linked up with the somewhat unconventional Nilton 'Filé' Petrone, who had previously performed miracles with Romário. Ronaldo worked tirelessly with the physiotherapist at his clinic in Barra da Tijuca, aiming to strengthen the knee to help with the explosive actions he was becoming famous for. Ronaldo combined leg exercises, trampolining and swimming. While recuperating, he told an interviewer, 'I need football, I need to score. Football for me, it's my life. If I cannot do this, then …' before tailing off. The brief exchange offered a glimpse into his almost desperate frame of mind at the time. The ever-present smile was absent whenever Ronaldo was unable to play. His return to competitive football came as a second-half substitute in a 2-1 defeat at Sparta Rotterdam in the penultimate league game of the season in late April.

Eleven days after the conclusion of the Eredivisie, PSV faced Sparta in Rotterdam again, this time with the KNVB Cup at stake. With PSV 3-1 up, Ronaldo replaced Nilis for the final 15 minutes, and although he didn't score he managed an assist as the match ended 5-2. His first trophy in European football was tinged with bitterness, however. It wasn't just the cup final omission alone that upset Ronaldo; he had the Olympics on his mind. Brazilian representatives were present in Rotterdam, hoping to assess his fitness ahead of the summer games, and he worried his lack of action would harm his chances of selection. 'It was a bad surprise when I found I was only a sub, but then Advocaat made me warm up for 35 minutes before putting me on,' Ronaldo told Dutch TV channel RTL 4 after the game. 'He and Frank Arnesen had been asking me constantly about whether I wanted to go to the Olympics, and I not only told them "yes" but that I needed to prove my fitness in this cup final. It's my impression that they didn't want me to go and play for Brazil in Atlanta and that's why I was left out. It's not being named a sub that angered me but when precisely it happened – when Brazilian federation staff had come to assess me.'

It was enough to make Ronaldo – who still managed 19 goals in 21 games in what was an injury-disrupted campaign – want to exit the club. 'When I joined PSV, they told me they'd not put barriers in my way if I wanted to leave because I was unhappy, and that's how I feel now,' the disgruntled young star said. A proud and defiant Advocaat hit back, 'The door is open for him to leave and never come back. His treatment of PSV is unacceptable and infantile.' Ronaldo replied, 'Advocaat has no idea about football and no idea how to treat people.'

Even at this stage of his career, the influence of Pitta and Martins was becoming clear. Would they have engineered a move anyway, and was this a handy ruse? Or would they have stayed at PSV if it weren't for the fallout at the final? 'When a player is as good as Ronaldo was, you knew he wasn't going to stay that long,' said Frans Claes, who also hinted at the control Ronaldo's entourage had over his career. 'I don't think he could make his own choices; he had managers who wanted to make money out of him.' At the time, Advocaat echoed similar sentiments, 'I don't think this desire to depart has anything to do with the cup final but that the vultures around him are using it as an excuse to force his departure.' Advocaat may ultimately feel vindicated by the decision given his side won the KNVB Cup. They also finished closer to Ajax in the league and saw a decent UEFA Cup run ended by Barcelona in the last eight. The manager was in a strong position.

* * *

Björn van der Doelen fondly remembers his time alongside Ronaldo in the PSV squad, 'He was incredible. He would run with the ball at his feet, and you'd think you could handle it, but it was almost like he had a turbo button. I played against him in training many times, the first XI against the rest. I often had to play as a defender because we didn't have enough defenders. He didn't do much and it was very easy until he decided to score and picked up the ball and started running. You couldn't stop him.' The Goirle-born midfielder was more than happy to do Ronaldo's dirty work, 'You don't mind running a few extra miles when you have a player like that in your team because he wasn't defending that much. Sometimes you'd yell at him that he must work a bit more but on the other hand, if we didn't play well, if we didn't concede, we knew he would score one or two goals and win us the game.'

For Van der Doelen, it was Ronaldo's laid-back demeanour that also made him unique, 'It seemed like he didn't get nervous before games, just really enjoyed playing football. He played like he was still a kid playing with friends. It was one of his strengths that he didn't think, he just played. He's the biggest talent I've ever seen, he was amazing. Ruud van Nistelrooy was mentally the strongest player I ever played with; he was also great. But Ronaldo was completely different, he played on intuition. Overall, by far the best player I ever played with.'

Like Ronaldo, Van der Doelen wouldn't stay at PSV for ever. The midfielder spent a season on loan in Belgium with Standard Liege in 1997/98, leaving the club permanently in 2001 before turning out for Twente and NEC. Van der Doelen – who represented the Netherlands up to under-21 level – retired in 2006. Despite his playing career, he wasn't interested in coaching after hanging up his boots, aside from helping his son's team for fun. Instead he became a musician, despite only picking up a guitar for the first time when he was 19. 'I needed to get out of football. It's a small world. It's nice to do something different to what I've done my whole life,' he reflected.

* * *

Arriving in the Netherlands as a boy, Ronaldo was well on his way to attaining superstar status. He had cemented himself in Brazil's plans and scored a hatful of goals in domestic and European competitions. As predicted by Romário, Dutch football had proven to be the perfect finishing school. Ronaldo joked that he would beat his compatriot's scoring record in the Netherlands, and was true to his word, with 54 goals in 57 matches. Now, another, even greater, challenge loomed.

Chapter 4

Heaven and Hell

THERE WAS little that veteran Barcelona manager Bobby Robson hadn't seen during his long life and illustrious career. From a mining community in England's north-east, a teenage Robson lived through the Second World War before enjoying a stellar professional playing career with Fulham and West Bromwich Albion. He made his name as a manager at Ipswich Town, winning an FA Cup and UEFA Cup. Success in Suffolk preceded an eight-year spell as England manager during which he witnessed first-hand Diego Maradona's cunning, and brilliance, in Mexico City's Estadio Azteca in 1986, and Paul Gascoigne's tears in Turin four years later at the subsequent World Cup. Spells with PSV Eindhoven, Sporting Lisbon, and Porto earned him a shot at the coveted manager's job, or poisoned chalice depending on your outlook, at the Camp Nou.

Yet there he was, on 12 October 1996, in the city of Santiago de Compostela – ironically the endpoint of a famous religious pilgrimage – looking like he had seen God himself. Standing near the Barcelona dugout, Robson was in utter disbelief at what he had just witnessed, his hands on his head, and then in the air, as if to say, 'How?'

In the tunnel before kick-off, Ronaldo was all smiles, confident, as if he knew what havoc he was about to wreak on the SD Compostela defence. The Brazilian set the tone in the first minute as William turned his cross into his net to give the *Blaugrana* the lead. Fifteen minutes later, a tricky and direct run set up his strike partner and compatriot Giovanni to double the visitors' advantage.

However, it was in the 36th minute that Ronaldo left his experienced coach stunned, well and truly announcing himself as a Barcelona player. Seizing control of the ball near the halfway line, Ronaldo maintained his balance despite the overzealous attention of Moroccan midfielder Saïd Chiba. Leaving more players in his wake using a combination of mesmerising close control and pace, he balletically danced in between two defenders before sliding the ball past the goalkeeper to make it 3-0.

Then came the trademark celebration. Wearing the iconic, sponsorless, Kappa shirt with red and blue stripes, and a gold chain protruding from the neck of his shirt, Ronaldo outstretched his arms – reminiscent of Rio's famous landmark, the Christ the Redeemer statue – then pumped his right fist. Even some of the home supporters, in a crowd of just 12,000, applauded the young genius. Although few saw it in the flesh, since then millions have watched the goal on YouTube.

One minute after the restart, Ronaldo made it 4-0, touching a delicately clipped pass from Luís Figo out of the reach of the defenders before a cool finish past the now-bewildered goalkeeper. The match ended in a 5-1 victory and Ronaldo took all the plaudits. If there were any doubts before, there were none now: the striker was a world star. 'You won't find a player who can score goals like that,' Robson said after the game. 'Can anybody, anywhere, show me a better player?'

The international press, and luminaries of the sport, were extolling the genius of the young Brazilian. The front page of *AS*, a Spanish daily football newspaper, led the following morning with the headline 'Pelé Has Returned', along with a caption suggesting Ronaldo had 'blown up' televisions across Spain. A graphic in the bottom-right corner demonstrated how he had scored the mind-boggling goal. 'It doesn't worry me,' said Ronaldo about the Pelé comparisons. 'It's good to be compared with the best players.' To his great credit, the player himself warned the *Jornal do Brasil*, 'I may not be the best in the world yet. But I'm going to be. It's wonderful to be compared to Pelé, but he is the king and I'm just at the start of my career.'

Nike later created an advert using footage of the goal, with the slogan, 'What if you asked God to make you the best soccer player in the world?' The referee that night, Victor Esquinas Torres, commented years after, 'I felt very satisfied with my own role in that goal. I could have blown for a foul on him several times, but I let him keep going and going … my goodness.' Spanish football expert Sid Lowe described it as a 'defining moment', comparing the forward to the seemingly unstoppable New Zealand rugby icon Jonah Lomu.

* * *

Despite the enormity of the institution of FC Barcelona, a beast akin to a national team given the complex historical and political situation in Spain, Robson's experience ensured he would not be overawed by the pressures of one of football's most sought-after posts. And although the 63-year-old's grasp of Spanish, let alone

Catalan, was non-existent, he had assistance. A young translator named José Mourinho, who had been at his side for the last four years in Portugal, was a quick learner who soon spoke Catalan, and over time his influence over coaching sessions increased.

The club Robson, Mourinho, and Ronaldo joined was divided by a toxic split. Johan Cruyff, who starred at the Camp Nou as a player in the 1970s and then managed the club with great success between 1988 and 1996, departed after two trophyless seasons. Pro- and anti-Cruyff factions could be found throughout the club, fanbase and media. To avoid any potential conflicts of interest, it was deemed best if Johan's son, Jordi – then on the Barcelona books – moved on. He reluctantly joined Manchester United.

A top striker became Robson's priority, with the assumption that a marquee name would distract unsatisfied fans from the Cruyff saga. Alan Shearer had starred for England in June, finishing top scorer at Euro '96 as the Three Lions went within an inch of Gascoigne's studs of reaching the Wembley final. Robson spoke with Shearer's manager, Blackburn Rovers' Ray Harford, who categorically told him the Geordie hitman was not for sale. The Shearer rejection led Robson down a different path. Speaking with Dutch defender Stan Valckx, whom Robson knew from his time with PSV and Sporting, the conversation turned to a young Brazilian striker. Valckx gave Ronaldo a glowing recommendation.

Robson hoped his PSV links would help facilitate the deal, although the Eindhoven outfit weren't feeling sentimental or charitable to their former manager; the initial offer of $10m for the 19-year-old was rejected. With Ronaldo halfway through a four-year contract, PSV played hardball, yet the breakdown of the relationship between Ronaldo and Dick Advocaat made his position at the Philips Stadion somewhat untenable. It was clear the transfer would happen; it was just a matter of when and for how much. PSV ultimately managed to extract $19.5m out of Barcelona, roughly double the opening bid. In breaking a world record that had stood for four years, Robson was putting all his eggs in the Ronaldo basket.

On 10 July, representatives from both clubs met in Eindhoven to finalise the deal. After completing a medical Ronaldo put pen to paper for eight years, with a salary of $1.5m per season. The player's agents, who knew how to squeeze a lemon, also had to factor in Ronaldo's image rights when negotiating the contract. The unveiling took place one week later, on 17 July in Miami, where Ronaldo was based ahead of the Atlanta Olympics. Despite his worries following the KNVB Cup Final – and subsequent argument with the management at PSV – he had been selected for the games in the United States. Accompanied by Joan Gaspart, the club's vice-president, Ronaldo posed for the cameras, holding the shirt and even kissing the badge. 'I feel very happy to be able to sign for Barça,' he told waiting journalists. PSV was a great place to test the waters of European football, but the kid gloves were off and Ronaldo was now at a bona fide behemoth of a club.

Three days after Ronaldo officially became a Barcelona player, the Olympic football tournament kicked off, with 16 teams competing across five cities. On 21 July Brazil lost 1-0 to Japan in Miami. Ronaldo came off the bench to replace Sávio, but he was unable to find the decisive goal. It was reported that Mário Zagallo was unhappy with the Ronaldo circus, feeling that his move to Barcelona was disrupting his preparations, and therefore started the star on the bench. Two days later, back in the Orange

Bowl, Brazil beat Hungary 3-1. Wearing the number 18 shirt, and then known as 'Ronaldinho' as there was an older Ronaldo in the squad, the forward opened the scoring. A long pass was hoisted over the top, the bounce beating the Hungary defender who misjudged the ball's movement. Ronaldo collected it gladly, taking one touch with his right foot before his second took him around the goalkeeper, sliding it into the empty net before the Hungarian defenders were able to stop him.

Brazil faced Nigeria in the final group game, once again in Miami. After 30 minutes Ronaldo scored the only goal, a left-footed strike from the edge of the penalty area. For the second game in a row he was replaced by Sávio. Given the heat, the short turnaround times between games, and his lack of football for PSV, it was sensible to use the squad. Brazil faced another African opponent in the quarter-final and after 53 minutes Ghana were 2-1 to the good. Middlesbrough's Juninho showed quick thinking when Brazil were awarded a free kick. While Ghana were organising themselves, the pint-sized playmaker placed the ball down and slid it to Ronaldo, who drilled it into the bottom corner to equalise. The Brazilians, in their blue shirts, celebrated while Ghana complained. If his first goal was somewhat controversial, the second was stunning. Showing the pace to beat the defence, Ronaldo opened his body and dinked the ball over the goalkeeper from a tight angle. Bebeto finished the scoring to send Brazil through relatively comfortably after the early scare.

The semi-final pitted Brazil against Nigeria's Super Eagles in a repeat of the group-stage clash. After 77 minutes Zagallo's men were cruising, then what followed was what the *LA Times* perhaps hyperbolically described as 'the worst 16 minutes in the history of Brazilian soccer'. Victor Ikpeba scored to make it 3-2;

after 85 minutes Ronaldo was replaced by Sávio. Several people suggested that this was a sign of Zagallo's complacency, although the coach said Ronaldo's knee was swelling up, and that he was being withdrawn as a precaution ahead of a potential final. That final never came. Two goals from Nwankwo Kanu – the winner coming as the 'golden goal' in extra time – gave Nigeria an historic victory in a seven-goal thriller. Ronaldo recovered sufficiently to participate in the third-place play-off match two days later, at the Sanford Stadium against Portugal. Showing little sign of a knee issue, he opened the scoring after four minutes – from another Juninho pass – as Brazil cruised to a 5-0 win. Ronaldo finished the tournament with a bronze medal for his efforts, and his total of five goals was just behind the haul of Argentinean striker Hernán Crespo and team-mate Bebeto.

* * *

Ronaldo arrived in Barcelona following an extended break after his Olympic exertions, mobbed at El Prat airport by excited fans. Fellow Brazilian Giovanni wasn't best pleased, 'I love Carnaval too, but as a professional my duty is to be here. A return journey to Brazil for the sake of two days – and with hard partying thrown in – is hard work. Even if I had the time off, I would have stayed here.'

* * *

Barcelona were comfortably beaten 4-0 away to Tenerife at the beginning of March, on a weekend in which Real Madrid won to extend their La Liga lead to nine points. Maximum points followed for Robson's charges in the three following matches, without conceding a goal; Ronaldo scored against Compostela and Sevilla. He then equalised in a 1-1 draw at Valencia.

In March, Barcelona welcomed Atlético Madrid to the Camp Nou for the second leg of the Copa del Rey quarter-final, the tie nicely poised after a 2-2 draw in the capital. The meeting produced a classic. With just half an hour on the clock, Milinko Pantić's hat-trick had given Atleti a shock 3-0 lead which they held until half-time. The white hankies were waved by the Catalan crowd. Robson's job hung in the balance. The under-fire coach reshaped the team, bravely withdrawing defensive players Gheorge Popescu and Laurent Blanc, replacing them with forwards Pizzi and Stoichkov. Lady luck must have been smiling on him because two minutes after the restart a Ronaldo volley made it 3-1; he soon had his second after a tap-in at the far post. The spirits were dampened a minute later when Pantić scored again but the home side refused to be deterred. Figo scored after 67 minutes with a stunning volley from 20 yards, then five minutes later Ronaldo equalised. Pizzi made it five to cap off the remarkable comeback.

Mundo Deportivo described the scenes as 'delirium'. So moved, club president Josep Lluís Núñez, sitting in the stands, cried. Also in the famous cathedral of football that night was Ajax boss Louis van Gaal. The official reason for his presence was that his side were imminently due to play Atlético in the Champions League. However, it was strongly expected even at that time that he would take over from the unfortunate Robson at the end of the season.

After a five-month break, the Cup Winners' Cup returned in March. Ronaldo scored in both legs as Barcelona beat AIK Solna 4-2 on aggregate to reach the final four. Cup form continued to produce positive results, with knockout football providing respite from the inconsistencies of the league campaign. In early April, Barcelona reached the Copa del Rey Final after a 7-0 aggregate win over Las Palmas, thanks in no small part to two Ronaldo goals in the first leg. Later that month, after a 2-0 win in Florence, Barcelona also reached a European final after dispatching Fiorentina.

In La Liga, Ronaldo scored in all four games as Barça racked up wins over Sporting Gijón, Atlético Madrid, and Athletic Bilbao, with the only negative result in the sequence being a 3-1 defeat at Real Valladolid. In the 5-2 win over Atleti at the Vicente Calderón Stadium, Ronaldo scored a hat-trick. In response to abuse from the club's ultras, he produced an obscene gesture known in Brazil as the 'banana'. Barcelona opened May with a 3-1 win in Extremadura, with one goal coming from Ronaldo. Going into the final *Clásico* of the season, Robson's side were eight points behind Capello's men. It was a must-win game to keep the faint title hopes alive. Just before half-time, Figo was felled in the box by Roberto Carlos. Ronaldo missed the resulting penalty but was able to turn in the rebound. It proved to be the winner and reduced the deficit to five points with the same number of games remaining in the league schedule.

Four days later Barça went into the Cup Winners' Cup Final in Rotterdam full of confidence. At De Kuip, where they'd lost to Manchester United in the final of the same cup six years earlier, Barcelona faced holders Paris Saint-Germain, who were looking to become the first club to retain the trophy. The French side boasted an XI featuring Brazilians Raí and Leonardo, who were backed up by a raft of French internationals. Towards the end of the first half the only goal of the game settled the tie. Luis Enrique passed the ball to Ronaldo, lurking ominously on the corner of the 18-yard box on the left-hand side. His first touch was uncharacteristically sloppy, but like a matador teasing a bull it encouraged Bruno N'Gotty to dive in with a reckless lunge.

Ronaldo got there first, his touch taking him beyond the defender. It was probably the easiest decision German referee Markus Merk had to give throughout his whole career. This time Ronaldo made no mistake, confidently side-footing the ball down the middle of the goal, just beyond the boot of Bernard Lama, who had dived to his right. Barcelona now had the Cup Winners' Cup to go with the Supercopa de España won at the start of the season.

Back on the domestic front, Ronaldo scored in a 3-1 win at Celta Vigo, then recorded his final goal for the club in a 1-0 home victory over Deportivo. It was vintage Ronaldo. On the floor after a tackle, the ball fell close to him. He rose to his feet and in almost one movement went past one Depor player before switching on the turbochargers to blast past another and finishing. It happened in the blink of an eye. With three league games to go, Robson's men had cut the lead of Capello's side to just two points. Although relegation-threatened Hércules shouldn't have posed much threat, they had already won at the Camp Nou, and Barcelona would have to travel to Alicante without their star man. Despite taking an early lead through Luis Enrique, they conceded twice, losing 2-1. *Los Griegos* ultimately failed to avoid the drop, despite their league double over Barcelona. Real Madrid won comfortably on the same weekend, extending their lead to five points with two games to go. The title race was all but over, and this weekend had been a key turning point.

While Barcelona were facing Hércules, Ronaldo and Brazil were in Lyon preparing for Le Tournoi, a friendly tournament hosted by France as part of its preparations for the World Cup the following summer. In the opening match, Roberto Carlos scored *that* free kick against *Les Bleus*, putting physics-defying swerve on the long-range strike. Next up were the Italians, Ronaldo scoring one in the thrilling 3-3 draw. Receiving the ball on the edge of the area, Ronaldo spun his defender, went past Alessandro Costacurta, then slid the ball in at Gianluca Pagliuca's near post, wrong-footing the Italian number one. Brazil beat England in their final fixture of the round-robin tournament, although the Three Lions topped the group and lifted the trophy. Le Tournoi was a sore point for Barcelona. For months they had argued with FIFA that as it wasn't an official tournament, Brazil had no right to demand Ronaldo's participation. FIFA sided with the Brazilians; the Barcelona hierarchy were apoplectic with rage. Ronaldo's club season was now over, with the *Seleção* hotfooting it from France to Bolivia for the Copa América.

Barcelona won their last two league games. However, Real Madrid's healthy lead meant they were still able to lose heavily to Celta Vigo and lift the league title with two points to spare. *Los Blancos*, without a European campaign to distract them, were refreshed and played a dozen fewer games than Barcelona during the season. The Copa del Rey Final, played against Real Betis at the Bernabéu at the end of June, was a welcome tonic for the Catalan giants, their third trophy of the campaign.

* * *

The day after Guardiola lifted the Spanish domestic cup, the 38th edition of the Copa América was concluding. Mário Zagallo's side made light work of Costa Rica in the opening match of group C. Leading 2-0 at half-time, Ronaldo – the second-youngest player in the squad – then scored a brace. His first goal was typical of his gifts. Reacting to a flick-on, he raced away from defenders before coolly finishing past the goalkeeper. For his second, he showed quick feet to dazzle the defender before shooting across the body of Erick Lonnis. Romário – who had just returned to the fold after two and a half years in the international wilderness and was now striking up a wonderful partnership with Ronaldo, dubbed 'Ro-Ro' – finished off the pummelling.

Wins over Mexico and Colombia meant Brazil sailed through the group stage with maximum points, giving them a plum quarter-final tie against one of the third-placed teams, Paraguay. Ronaldo put his side one up against their neighbours, demonstrating blistering pace and an accurate finish. No man alive could have stopped him and he enjoyed the celebrations, dancing with Romário. His second came after a jinking run from Denílson, the only player in the squad younger than Ronaldo, and who would surpass him as the world's most expensive footballer a little under 12 months later. Legendary goalkeeper José Luis Chilavert repelled a Ronaldo penalty in the second half but that was a small consolation for Paraguay in a game Brazil won with relative ease. In the semi-final, Brazil destroyed Peru 7-0. Ronaldo failed to get on the scoresheet and was replaced by Edmundo on 66 minutes.

From the lowlands of Santa Cruz, where Brazil had played all their games so far, the squad travelled to the harsh high altitude of La Paz for the final against the hosts. It was a city that had been unkind to Brazil in the past; in 1993 they lost a World Cup qualifier there. Using the conditions to their advantage, Bolivia had won all five games so far, defeating Venezuela, Peru, Uruguay, Colombia and Mexico en route to the final. After 79 minutes they were holding Brazil, too, in the Estadio Hernando Siles, having hit the bar several times and forced smart saves from Cláudio Taffarel. Then Ronaldo struck, smashing the ball into the top corner from the edge of the area. Substitute Zé Roberto wrapped things up with a late goal to make it 3-1.

Brazil had planned to reduce Bolivia's advantage by playing the game at a pedestrian pace as possible and flying into La Paz shortly before the game before the effects of high altitude had time to take their toll. It worked. The genius of Ronaldo – the tournament's top scorer – also helped, although it wasn't easy for the Phenomenon. 'There was no air,' he complained. 'I couldn't breathe. It was terrible.' It was Brazil's fifth Copa América, the first outside their borders, and they became the first South American team to hold the continental trophy and World Cup simultaneously. They were kings of the continents. And what made it more impressive was that after every game, the Brazil squad had enjoyed the after-dark delights of the Bolivian capital. Although it was hardly the post-match recovery the doctor ordered, it worked wonders for team spirit.

* * *

Despite league heartbreak, Robson's side had lifted three trophies in one season. The veteran English manager, however, was perhaps always on a hiding to nothing, having to follow in Johan Cruyff's footsteps. It was such a tumultuous campaign that a young lawyer named Joan Laporta established the 'Blue Elephant' group to protest the club's president. Robson faced criticism about his style of play – including from Ronaldo. The Englishman also spent most of the season acting as a middleman between the club hierarchy on one side, and Ronaldo and his representatives on the other. Speculation continually swirled that Louis van Gaal would be filling his shoes at the end of the season regardless of what happened. When the Dutchman inevitably took over, Robson was moved upstairs. He spent a year enjoying life on the Mediterranean, scouting players. His official title was director of signings; he recommended Rivaldo. Robson left the club altogether in 1998, returning to PSV.

Speaking in 2003, in a documentary aired to celebrate Robson's 70th birthday, Ronaldo spoke warmly about his former manager. 'As a trainer without doubt he is one of the greatest in the world,' the Brazilian said. 'The best thing about him is his personality, his character – which is brilliant. With him you can talk about anything and everything and he has the ability to put a smile on your face. He is a fantastic man. He was like a father to me. Bobby Robson helped me to be consistent and helped me a lot with my career. To be playing for a club like Barcelona at the tender age of 20 is not easy at all; Bobby Robson helped me to deal with this pressure.'

It can be argued that no other manager saw Ronaldo at a greater height of performance than Robson. Although he couldn't fire his team to La Liga glory, Ronaldo won the coveted Pichichi award, finishing on 34 league goals, nine more than the nearest challenger, Alfonso. His total haul in all competitions was 47 in 49 games, a remarkable number in an era before Lionel Messi and Cristiano Ronaldo ripped up the rule book and made one goal per game the norm.

The fact that Luis Enrique was overwhelmingly voted as player of the year by the club's supporters, however, shows that despite Ronaldo's phenomenal individual displays, and the three trophies gleaned in 1996/97, there always existed an uneasy relationship between player and club. October saw the beginning of a two-month spell in which he struggled for fitness and form, blaming the club's medical staff for being unable to give him the supposedly superior treatment on offer back home in Rio. Ronaldo criticised the club's fans for waving the white hankies in December and the numerous flights back home around the turn of the year – some of which were for physio sessions, but he undoubtedly enjoyed some of the city's famous nightlife while he was meant to be recuperating – would have done little to help his physical preparation or relations with the club's management team.

Then there was Le Tournoi, the friendly tournament that Barcelona did not want Ronaldo to partake in. The straw that broke the camel's back. Although he had little say after FIFA's insistence, it reinforced the idea that his heart was not with the club. And although Barcelona should have beaten the ultimately relegated Hércules in his absence, it was most certainly a distraction. 'Less Ronaldo and more Hércules,' said Pep Guardiola before the damaging defeat. 'For a long time, we've been going on about renovations, contracts ... let's talk about football.'

Perhaps the biggest issue throughout his year-long stay in Catalonia, however, was his contract, as alluded to in Guardiola's comment. It all began just months into the eight-year deal penned upon his arrival from PSV, rumbling on all season until it reached its unseemly conclusion in June 1997. As he adapted effortlessly to La Liga, the club worried that the release clause – which every player signed to a top Spanish club must have in their contract – was far too low to deter would-be suitors. Equally, Ronaldo's representatives – who were mockingly dubbed the 'Dalton Brothers' in the Spanish press, named after a gang of armed robbers in the US's Wild West – felt they had underplayed their hand and could extract a greater salary out of Barcelona's money men.

On 26 May, after months of arduous toing and froing, Ronaldo's representatives, or 'business associates' as he often referred to them, met Josep Núñez and Joan Gaspart at the Camp Nou to thrash out the final terms of the proposed new deal. A delighted Núñez emerged from the meeting, jubilantly claiming, 'He's ours for life.' The nine-year agreement effectively doubled Ronaldo's wages, as well as doubling the buyout clause. Both sides had the security they craved. Large crowds waited outside the stadium, expecting an end to the saga.

However, the following day, all hell broke loose. When the meeting reconvened to finalise the proposed deal, the truce collapsed. It's all but impossible to know which side was to blame. Bobby Robson claimed that Ronaldo's people – Reinaldo Pitta, Alexandre Martins and a third agent, Italian Giovanni Branchini – wanted a bonus from the club for their part in the negotiations. Ronaldo's entourage believed that the club were going back on their word, reneging on agreements reached the day before. 'It's all over,' said Núñez. 'Ronaldo is going.' Unsurprisingly Ronaldo, in Norway on international duty, sided with his camp, 'Everything Núñez has said is a lie and we no longer need to negotiate with them. He tells me one thing and my agents something else. He has been cheating us for seven months. It's sad, but I'm leaving.'

It was no secret that Inter president Massimo Moratti was a long-standing admirer of the Brazilian. Moratti – whose father Angelo was at the helm during Helenio Herrera's *Grande Inter* reign in the mid-1960s – was desperate to emulate his success, spending the family's oil money in pursuit of trophies. After the prolonged success of their greatest rivals, AC Milan, Moratti was keen to play catch up. 'It was a massive statement of what Moratti wanted to do,' said Richard Hall, who works for Inter on their English-language content.

On 20 June, Moratti Junior got his man. Ronaldo's lawyers, having received payment from Inter, deposited a cheque at La Liga's Madrid HQ that covered the release clause in his contract of just shy of £20m. 'Ronaldo is a costly present to Inter fans,' said Moratti. 'I'm sure it will pay off.' Initially, there was some confusion as to whether the buyout clause applied to clubs outside Spain, but the deal eventually happened.

Ronaldo became the second player – after Diego Maradona – to become the world's most expensive player twice, and it had happened within the space of a year. The reported figures vary, but the annual wage agreed was thought to be around £4m per season at the San Siro, with a hefty signing-on fee for him and his agents included in the long-term contract. 'I am very happy,' Ronaldo said from Bolivia. 'This is a problem that has been affecting the national team and now it is out of the way.'

Speaking in 1998 to Jimmy Burns, author of *Barça: A People's Passion*, Robson was in a reflective mood, although it was easy to detect the disappointment in his tone, 'I have nothing but admiration for that player, the fastest thing I've ever seen running with the ball – a great *chico*. But how was it possible that having bought the finest, best goalscorer in the world at a cost of $20m, we let him go one year later? How did anyone let it happen? Nobody here has had the courtesy to sit down and explain this to me.' Ronaldo had conquered the Dutch and Spanish leagues and now it was time for his biggest challenge: the number one league in the world, home to the meanest defences on the planet.

Chapter 5

Il Fenónemo

INTER SOON understood exactly what 'Ronaldomania' was, before the season had even begun. At the club's Appiano Gentile training centre, to the north-west of Milan, 4,000 fans turned up, waiting hours in the blistering summer heat to watch their new star being put through his paces after his three-week summer holiday. He'd only arrived in the country the day before, accompanied by Susana Werner, now his fiancée. A day later, in the Pirelli Cup, a pre-season friendly tournament sponsored by the tyre company whose name adorned Inter's black-and-blue-striped shirts, Ronaldo made his debut against Manchester United, playing 17 minutes in front of 60,000 fans in the San Siro. After the protracted transfer saga, *Interisti* could begin to get excited.

At this point, 40,000 season tickets had been sold, with another 20,000 expected to be snapped up in the month before the league campaign began. This was a massive increase on the 16,000 sold the previous season. Shirts with 'Ronaldo 10' on the back were selling as fast as they could be printed. Luigi 'Gigi' Simoni – the veteran coach who had achieved several promotions to the Italian top flight – was the man tasked with leading the new-look Inter side, replacing axed Englishman Roy Hodgson.

But after 80 minutes of the season-opener at home to Brescia, it looked like the start of another year of disappointment with the visitors leading through Dario Hübner. However, the relatively unknown Uruguayan Álvaro Recoba, a fellow new signing and debutant, stepped up with a dramatic and stunning brace, ironically overshadowing Ronaldo but getting 1997/98 off to a good start with three points.

September gleaned three wins out of three in Serie A, with Ronaldo scoring in each. Inter hit four at a rainy Bologna on matchday two, where in the 52nd minute Ronaldo made the first downpayment on Moratti's large outlay. Drifting between the full-back and the right centre-half, the Brazilian received a Youri Djorkaeff pass on the edge of the 18-yard box with his back to goal. Taking a touch, he spun inside and then finished to the goalkeeper's right when most would have gone across the body and into the far corner. The French midfielder later described their partnership. 'We had an almost perfect understanding,' said Djorkaeff. 'We have this intuition and can anticipate the other's movements. This comes from having the same spirit of playing the game that we both had when we were kids.'

The following weekend, Inter hosted Fiorentina, a match which was billed as Ronaldo versus Gabriel Batistuta, the South American pair vying for the unofficial title of the world's best striker. The *Viola*'s Argentine hitman was a few shy of 100 Serie A goals since joining in 1991 and had started the season on fire, with five in the first two games. In a fiery match, with a fervent atmosphere providing the backdrop, Ronaldo – the new kid on the block – opened the scoring in the 45th minute, latching on to a Diego Simeone pass to slide the ball under the goalkeeper from ten yards. Fiorentina equalised before the half-time whistle, then took the lead after the break through Batistuta. Inter ultimately won the fierce battle 3-2.

The following Saturday night, under the floodlights, Ronaldo grabbed a brace on the road as Inter comfortably dealt with relegation candidates Lecce, winning 5-1. With the score at 1-1, his first was a long-range free kick; his second came in the 80th minute of the emphatic victory. Significantly, despite being more than 1,000km to the south of Milan, Ronaldo was mobbed before the game. 'It wasn't just a signing for Inter; it was a signing for Serie A,' affirmed Inter's English-language content man Richard Hall. Within weeks the Italian press bestowed upon him the *Il Fenónemo* nickname that stuck with him throughout his career.

Inter ended the month with a 2-0 away win against Neuchâtel Xamax, sealing their passage to the second round of the UEFA Cup with a 4-0 aggregate score. Ronaldo had scored in the first leg against the Swiss side at the San Siro to send them on their way. On 5 October, Lazio took the lead before a 41st-minute Ronaldo penalty ensured the spoils were shared in the Serie A clash. In the middle of the month, Inter travelled to Piacenza for the first leg of the Coppa Italia last-16 tie after the Nerazzurri had dealt with Foggia in the previous round. Ronaldo scored twice in the first half and shared a tender moment with an awestruck ball boy on the way to the changing room at the break. The goal that sealed his hat-trick was a stunner that encapsulated all his strengths – picking up the ball from deep, close control, then a calm finish in front of the goalkeeper once the defence had been eliminated. Even though Piacenza won the second leg, Inter progressed to the quarter-final.

On 1 November, Inter beat Parma 1-0 at the San Siro. After 15 minutes it was Ronaldo with the only goal of the game, his free kick flying over the wall then dipping before kissing the crossbar on the way into the net. Three weeks later they were the nominated home team for the first Milan derby of the season. Ronaldo scored a penalty – awarded by Pierluigi Collina in front of a packed San Siro – in a 2-2 draw. Ronaldo also played a major part in Inter's opener, finished by Simeone, after almost appearing to be running in fast-forward mode in the build-up.

The following week Inter won 3-1 at Vicenza. Ronaldo's goal – scored after racing away from the defence on to a through ball – sealed the victory. On 6 December the Brazilian scored Inter's goal in a 1-1 draw at Sampdoria, playing a one-two with Simeone before slamming the ball in at Fabrizio Ferron's near post from the edge of the box. Three days later, Inter faced Strasbourg in the second leg of the last 16 of the UEFA Cup, having dumped out Lyon in the previous round. The Italians were 2-0 down from the first leg and needed a big performance at the San Siro to reach the quarter-final but when Ronaldo missed an early penalty it seemed that their luck was out. However, his long-range strike after 27 minutes made up for it, sending Inter on their way to a 3-0 win.

* * *

After the Strasbourg match, Ronaldo jetted off to Riyadh in Saudi Arabia to join his international colleagues for the first official Confederations Cup, missing Inter games against Roma and Udinese. Previously known as the King Fahd Cup, the tournament under the unforgiving desert sun was now a designated FIFA competition, meaning the participants were obliged to field a strong team. This was no problem for Brazil. With no qualification to worry about ahead of France '98, the world champions were keen to put on a good show, as they had done in Le Tournoi and the Copa América in the summer of 1997. These tournaments were the only competitive football they were getting between World Cups and acted as important dress rehearsals. As a show of unity, all the Brazil players shaved their heads ahead of the first match. Ronaldo kept his powder dry in the group stage, failing to score in three appearances. Mário Zagallo put his quiet performances down to the pressure he was under at club level. His team-mates, however, came to the fore and Brazil topped the table with seven points.

It was in the semi-final against the Czech Republic that Ronaldo came alive. In a tough game against the beaten finalists of the 1996 European Championship, the score remained goalless at half-time. Romário and then Ronaldo – tapping in a Denílson cross from the left – grabbed second-half goals to earn a place in the final. 'We had perfect synchronicity and it was fantastic,' Ronaldo said about partnering Romário. It was to get even better.

The final against Australia was to be no repeat of the drab goalless draw the two teams shared in the group phase. 'Having surprised the Brazilians once it was not going to happen again,' wrote Terry Venables in his 2014 autobiography *Born to Manage*. Their task was made even harder when Mark Viduka was red-carded in the 24th minute. Ronaldo and Romário ran riot, each scoring a hat-trick in a 6-0 mauling of the Socceroos. The record-breaking *Seleção* were the first team to simultaneously be world champions, continental champions, and hold the Confederations Cup title. For his four goals in the knockout stage, Ronaldo was awarded the bronze shoe, although he somehow failed to make the all-star team. By the end of 1997 the much-travelled forward had played more than 70 games on several continents throughout the calendar year.

* * *

The *Nerazzurri* had topped the Serie A table going into the winter break, and the domestic title challenge was looking promising. However Ronaldo fired blanks in January, failing to score as Inter picked up seven points from 12 upon resumption of the league campaign. Embarrassingly, Inter exited the Coppa Italia after a soul-destroying 5-0 first-leg mauling at the hands of rivals AC Milan. During his barren run Ronaldo travelled to FIFA's gala at Disneyland Paris on 12 January and was named their World Player of the Year, becoming the first player to retain the accolade. The gong could sit on his mantlepiece alongside the Ballon d'Or he picked up two days before Christmas. With the World Cup looming, it was undebatable that the explosive forward was the best player on the planet.

Ronaldo scored in a 1-0 win at Brescia in February, heading into an empty net after a cross had sailed over the goalkeeper's head. It was his first league goal in almost two months, although he turned provider in a crucial game, assisting Djorkaeff's goal in a 1-0 win over Juventus. The following match, a 1-1 draw in Florence, saw Ronaldo and Batistuta once again go head-to-head. Inter's Brazilian drew first blood, lashing a free kick past Francesco Toldo; Fiorentina's prolific Argentine equalised before half-time. Curiously, a couple of months earlier in Marseille's Stade Velodrome, the pair partnered each other in attack for a World XI against a European XI, a bizarre mid-season friendly which coincided with the draw for the group stage of the World Cup, featuring players from the 32 nations that would be represented at France '98.

Ronaldo scored a hat-trick in a 5-0 demolition of Lecce at the San Siro. He opened the scoring after a one-two with Simeone, then made it four when he scored a penalty in the 70th minute. His third, Inter's fifth, was an instinctive close-range header after the goalkeeper parried a shot into his path. Against Napoli, Ronaldo got one from the penalty spot after being fouled himself, in a 2-0 home win. At the beginning of March, Inter welcomed Schalke to the San Siro for the UEFA Cup quarter-final first leg. After defeat to the Germans on penalties in the final of the same competition the previous year, revenge was on the cards, and Ronaldo proved to be Inter's ace in the pack. Controlling a pass with his back to goal, he held off a defender before playing a vertical ball into Djorkaeff. Continuing his run, Ronaldo took the ball off the toes of the Frenchman, ghosting past two defenders before blasting the ball into the top corner with his left foot. A 1-1 draw in Germany sent them through to the final four.

After defeat away to Parma, Inter thumped Atalanta 4-0 at the San Siro with Ronaldo getting their third goal. Then another Milan derby loomed. Sandwiched between a Simeone brace, Ronaldo scored in the 77th minute. Francesco Moriero looped a ball into his path from wide on the right and as the ball bounced, Ronaldo half volleyed over Sebastiano Rossi's head from 15 yards. Another league victory followed, with Vicenza edged out at the San Siro by a stoppage-time penalty from Ronaldo.

Two more league wins produced three Ronaldo goals. The first, after rounding the goalkeeper in trademark fashion, came in a 3-0 win at home to Sampdoria. Then he scored a brace in a 2-1 win over Roma at the Stadio Olimpico. Ronaldo opened the scoring before compatriot Cafu equalised for the *Giallorossi*. Fortune was with Ronaldo for the second goal as his attempt to once again take the ball around the Roma custodian was foiled but it fell kindly into his path. After the game, Roma full-back

Vincent Candela was asked if there was any way to stop the striker. 'Call the *Carabinieri* [Italian police force],' was his response.

After a 2-1 first-leg victory at the San Siro against Spartak Moscow, Inter headed to Russia for the UEFA Cup semi-final second leg. Ronaldo produced one of his best performances in an Inter shirt, dazzling on a pitch of mud and sand. Grass was as sparse as sunlight in freezing Moscow on an afternoon so cold that even the home players wore woolly gloves. Spartak went a goal ahead after 12 minutes, levelling the aggregate score to lead the tie on away goals. Ronaldo opportunistically equalised, poking home as the ball bounced around in the six-yard box. However, the second was pure magic. Controlling a throw-in from Luigi Sartor on his thigh, Ronaldo spun, playing a one-two with Iván Zamorano. In one touch he took out two Spartak defenders and, for the umpteenth time that season, went round the goalkeeper before scoring in an empty net. It was a stunning, rapid-fire goal that seemingly came out of nothing, and was even more impressive considering the surface it was scored on. 'Ronaldo was out of this world,' said Inter season ticket holder and memorabilia collector Ciaran Crilly.

A 2-0 home win over Udinese was Inter's sixth on the bounce in Serie A. Goalless with ten minutes remaining, Djorkaeff scored before Ronaldo closed the show with a thumping free kick from the edge of the area. The player, and his club, were both flying. But then came the match that, to many, would define the season as well as an era in Italian football in which Juventus were perceived to have received favourable treatment from match officials.

Inter travelled to Turin just one point behind the rampant league leaders, who had barely dropped points since losing at the San Siro in January. This Derby d'Italia would have significant ramifications in the title race and although the *Nerazzurri* had not won the Scudetto for almost a decade, with Ronaldo leading the attack many thought this was their year. Despite the plethora of talent on display at the Stadio Delle Alpi, however, it was referee Piero Ceccarini who grabbed the headlines. Alessandro Del Piero gave the Old Lady the lead after 21 minutes, with the home side heading into the break with a slender advantage. The first half was aggressive, forcing Ceccarini to repeatedly use his whistle, but it was nothing compared to what was to follow in the second period. The cynicism and scuffles broke up play, suiting Juve who were content to hold on for a classic Italian scoreline of 1-0. Lippi made defensive changes while Simoni rolled the dice. The Inter boss had no choice.

In the 69th minute the ball fell to Ronaldo in the box. Danger. He poked it around Mark Iuliano with his right foot and the Juve defender clattered into him, sending Ronaldo to the ground. It was a blatant body check although if you're being overly generous to Iuliano, you could argue he had nowhere to go, and the clash was an inevitable coming together. Ceccarini waived away the Inter claims and all hell broke loose. Simoni was sent to the stands, while being restrained by police, for his remonstration at the referee's questionable decision. Less than a minute later, with the whiff of chaos and carnage lingering in the air, Juve broke at the other end. Edgar Davids found Zinedine Zidane, who found Del Piero in the opposite penalty area. The Italian golden boy came together with Taribo West and went to ground easily in the presence of the Nigerian defender. This time Ceccarini awarded a penalty. Although Gianluca Pagliuca saved Del Piero's 12-yard effort, it didn't dampen Inter's sense of injustice. There was still time for more drama in a match that was watched by millions in the UK on Channel 4's *Football Italia*; Inter had a goal disallowed when Zamorano was adjudged to have fouled Juve goalkeeper Angelo Peruzzi.

The game finished 1-0 and the pendulum swung in favour of Juve who now held a four-point advantage with nine to play for. The row rumbled on for days. Many suggested it was one in a long line of refereeing decisions that had favoured Juve, who were later implicated in *Calciopoli*, a match-fixing scandal uncovered in 2006 that saw them punished with relegation to Serie B. The press used words such as 'shameful' and politicians had to be separated to prevent a brawl after arguments erupted, leading to the suspension of parliament.

Simoni, Zamorano, Brazilian midfielder Zé Elias and Ronaldo were among those handed bans for their protests. 'The league can punish me, but I can't stay quiet today,' Ronaldo said after the game. 'The whole world can see that the officials were in favour of Juve. I can't go on like this. Football is joy when you play 11 against 11, but it becomes sadness if you play 11 against 12.' Simoni said, 'There should be an inquiry because this situation is quite incredible.' Juve general manager Luciano Moggi responded to the forward's comments, 'Ronaldo's a good lad on the pitch, but less so when he says this sort of stuff. He really shouldn't go stirring things up.'

In 2016, Ceccarini doubled down, 'I still believe that contact [on Ronaldo] was not punishable by a penalty kick. Gigi Simoni always talks about me and I could even press charges on him for what he's been saying. I wouldn't give that penalty even if I were under torture. Unfortunately, there are some articles you can find on the internet suggesting I admitted the mistake. That's not true. Images show that it is Ronaldo who hit Iuliano, not the other way around. I was on the pitch, just a few metres away from the scene. The defender wants to stop the striker's run, but Ronaldo moves the ball and doesn't follow it. He hits Iuliano who is still in the middle of the area. I told Pagliuca that would have been a charging foul in basketball. Actually, I should have probably given a free kick for Juventus.'

A deflated Inter followed the disappointment with a goalless draw at home to Piacenza, although Juve also drew 0-0 on the same day. Two games to go, and there were still four points in it.

The UEFA Cup Final – the first in the competition's history to be played as a one-off match – proved a welcome distraction, although Inter couldn't escape domestic football in some sense: they faced Lazio at the Parc des Princes. Free from the pressure of the title race, however, Inter were excellent, producing one of their best performances of the season. For many it was the highlight of Ronaldo's time with the club. Zamorano, who missed a penalty in the shoot-out of the previous year's final, exorcised his demons by opening the scoring in Paris after just five minutes. The relief on the face of the Chilean was palpable. Iconic Argentinean Javier Zanetti made it two on the hour with a wonder strike that sliced off his right boot and hit the bar on its way to nestling in the net. In the 70th minute Ronaldo, who had earlier cracked a shot off the crossbar, made it 3-0. Latching on to a pass from Moriero, the Brazilian beat the offside trap to race into acres of space. Face to face with Lazio's Luca Marchegiani, Ronaldo dropped his shoulder, feinting to go left, before shifting his body and going to the right. It was vintage Ronaldo.

As strange as it sounds, perhaps Ronaldo's most memorable contribution to the game wasn't even a goal, and it occurred in his half, close to the touchline. He toyed with numerous Lazio players, displaying the full repertoire of tricks. Impeccable footwork then an 'elastico' embarrassed substitute Guerino Gottardi, before Ronaldo slipped by the lunging Matías Almeyda. It's a passage of play that has been widely shared and viewed millions of times. Later in the game, with the 'olé' chants ringing around the Parc des Princes, Ronaldo drew a foul from a frustrated Almeyda, who received his second yellow card and was sent for an early bath. It was a memorable night against a strong Lazio team – managed by Sven-Gorän Eriksson – containing the likes of Pierluigi Casiraghi, Roberto Mancini, Pavel Nedvěd, and Vladimir Jugović. They had won the Coppa Italia the week before so were no strangers to big cup occasions. But Ronaldo and Inter were inspired.

A subplot of the final narrative was a battle between Ronaldo, widely regarded as the most fearsome forward on the planet, against Alessandro Nesta, one of Italy's finest defenders. This time there was no doubt who came out on top. 'It was the worst experience of my career,' said Nesta, who watched the final back to see how he could have done better until he realised how futile an exercise it was. 'Ronaldo was simply unstoppable.' Ronaldo was delighted, 'We played very well and deserved the victory: we didn't make a mistake from the first minute to the last. I'm happy because this is my first trophy with Inter. It was great to win in Paris; I will return here with my national team and give my all to win the World Cup too.'

Richard Hall believes it was Ronaldo's best moment in an Inter shirt, 'The Lazio game was the high point. When Ronaldo goes round Marchegiani and slots it in, fantastic.' Ciaran Crilly, who was in the Parc des Princes, concurs, 'The performance of Ronaldo that evening in Paris was out of this world. Here was the best player in the world playing his best game. The triumph was glorious in the history of Inter. Everything about it was glorious – from the special third shirt for the UEFA Cup matches through to that performance in the final. In that era, there was never a more complete and dominant performance in a European final. It is easy to look at it through a modern lens. However, you also need to understand the importance of the UEFA Cup to Inter at the time; in the 1990s, Inter thought the UEFA Cup was theirs. After winning it in 1991 and 1994, the loss in 1997 was hard-hitting and very controversial. There was a lot of ill feeling after the second leg against Schalke, so winning the UEFA Cup in 1998 was therapeutic.'

Despite the European triumph, the domestic hangover from the emotionally draining Juve match remained. Ronaldo gave Inter the lead after 34 minutes against Bari but the home side scored two late goals to seal the win and hand the title to Juventus, who beat Bologna in Turin. On the final day of the season, Inter beat Empoli 4-1 at the San Siro with Ronaldo scoring twice. He finished the season with 25 Serie A goals, although it wasn't enough to win the prestigious Capocannoniere title, which went to Oliver Bierhoff, Udinese's German striker, who notched 27.

Ronaldo scored 34 in 47 games in all competitions, an excellent individual return for the Italian Footballer of the Year. When he landed in Italy the previous summer he said he wanted to prove he could do it in the tightest league in the world, one that became synonymous with solid defences, and he certainly did. It was the glamour league at the time, with wealthy owners and the world's best coaches and players, and was arguably at its peak in the mid-to-late-1990s. But for Ronaldo, it was just football. 'His first season was an absolute success,' said Ciaran Crilly. 'Over the past 15 years or so, people have debated who is the best player in the world out of Lionel Messi and Cristiano Ronaldo. In 1998, there was only one.'

With Juve drawing their last fixture, the final deficit was five points and second-placed Inter qualified for the 1998/99 Champions League. Despite the domestic disappointment, it was Inter's first genuine title challenge for a decade, and there was massive optimism for the future. The European trophy gave Ronaldo a taste of success in Paris that he could only hope to continue with his national team as Brazil geared up to defend their World Cup in France.

Chapter 6

The Ghost of Paris

IN MARCH 1998, during the build-up to the World Cup in France, American sports giant Nike released one of the greatest and most talked about TV adverts of all time. Much of its beauty lay in the simplicity of its concept: bored professional footballers stuck in the airport, waiting for yet another flight, the less glamorous side of the game. The crucial ingredient, which brought the advert to life, was the Brazilian tendency to turn something so mundane into a party. The result was *Airport 98*.

The advert begins with a frustrated squad bemoaning their delayed flight. Then a bag is unzipped and a ball is produced. Suddenly the lethargic players come to life. The star of the show, Ronaldo, starts the proceedings. The players perform flicks and tricks, evading security guards and other travellers. Romário kicks a ball through the X-ray machine and then down a jetway, with the action moving to the runway – where the scenes were shot in 45°C heat. A plane passes by, with fellow Nike athlete Eric Cantona occupying a window seat. He spots what is happening outside, shrugs, and then goes back to his magazine as if it is the most normal thing in the world.

Back inside the terminal building, the advert ends with whom it began: Ronaldo. With fellow passengers cheering him on, he takes the ball past several team-mates with an array of skills before shooting on a makeshift goal. Onlookers hold their breath, the ball hits the post, and Ronaldo puts his hands to his head. Then the advert fades to black with just the Nike swoosh visible. If you believe in that sort of thing, looking back you'd be forgiven for thinking it was some kind of premonition ahead of the tournament.

Backed by a soundtrack of Sérgio Mendes's version of the classic samba hit 'Mas Que Nada', the advert was directed by Hollywood filmmaker John Woo, best known for the 1997 blockbuster *Face/Off* starring John Travolta and Nicholas Cage. Woo later explained he wanted 'to produce a musical commercial that showed the beauty and energy of the players and the product'. He encouraged improvisation, something which, when it comes to football, is second nature to Brazilians. 'It was fun,' said Ronaldo. 'It was like being in an action movie. John Woo gave us crazy ideas.'

The bulk of the filming took place in Rio's Galeão airport during the festive period in 1997, with the final scene shot at Milan's Malpensa airport in January. On 25 March the advert premiered worldwide, except for Argentina. It was felt that the nation of Brazil's footballing arch rivals would be less than enamoured with the work. Working alongside long-time collaborator, advertising and marketing agency Wieden+Kennedy, Nike plunged over £20m into the tournament in France. It was part of their fight against Adidas, who traditionally had the World Cup market cornered, an attempt to usurp the German company to become the number one soccer brand on the planet. In the same month the advert premiered, Nike also released the Mercurial, the super lightweight boot which was tailored specifically around Ronaldo's speed and style of play. It was football's equivalent of Nike's Air Jordan range.

At this point Ronaldo was one of the most marketable athletes on the planet, in the same league as the likes of Michael Jordan and Tiger Woods. On 25 January, during the Super Bowl between Green Bay Packers and Denver Broncos, Nike debuted a new advert. Sixty seconds of airtime for a cool $2.6m. Several stars, including Ronaldo, bared all, covered up with the help of clever lighting and shadowing, ironically to sell clothes. The inference was that Nike's athletic apparel acts almost as a second skin, allowing people to compete more comfortably and with a high level of performance in a range of sports.

In December 1996, Nike signed a ten-year, $200m deal with the penniless Brazilian Football Confederation (CBF). Ronaldo later inked a decade-long agreement worth $1.5m a year. 'I think he is changing the game of soccer the way that Michael Jordan changed the game of basketball,' Nike's Joaquin Hidalgo said at the time. 'We know for a fact that he is the most global of all athletes today, bar none.' Nike later teamed up with Inter to manufacture their shirts, a long-term deal thought to be worth more than $100m. With Umbro out of the picture, Ronaldo would not be seen in anything other than Nike. He was like a pop star, mobbed everywhere he went. Now he was expected to take the World Cup by storm.

* * *

France, who edged out Morocco in the bidding process, were hosting their first World Cup in 60 years. Brazil qualified as holders and had to use tournaments such as Le Tournoi, the Copa América and the Confederations Cup to sharpen their skills. The biggest selection controversy by coach Mário Zagallo was the omission of Romário. He and Ronaldo, the 'Ro-Ro' partnership, had been performing well together, scoring 13 goals between them in internationals during 1997. They enjoyed a good rapport on and off the pitch and it was expected they would take that form into the World Cup. However, on 2 June, the fiery forward was sent home from the squad's training camp. 'I am very sad but we must have even greater determination,' said Ronaldo. All the pressure now fell on the young striker's shoulders. 'If you look at the games Brazil played in 1997, he and Romário were flying,' said Brazilian journalist and author Fernando Duarte. 'They were dominating. It suddenly became Ronaldo's job to carry Brazil.'

As holders, Brazil participated in the curtain-raiser, following a spectacular and colourful – yet unusually short – opening ceremony. The game, on 10 June, took place in the brand-new Stade de France, an 80,000-capacity arena in the Paris suburb of Saint-Denis. For Scotland manager Craig Brown there were no pre-match nerves. He had formed part of the coaching staff at the 1986 and 1990 World Cups, as well as leading his country at Euro '96, where they faced a massive challenge in hosts and rivals England. 'I was concerned about the opposing team, but not afraid or nervous,' said a positive Brown. 'I was never nervous, I'm not a nervous kind of guy. I know we were playing the world champions, but I was quietly confident that we could give a good account of ourselves. I was optimistic we'd do well because we'd had a good qualification campaign – in ten games we only conceded three goals. To open the World Cup in France against the champions wasn't a daunting task; it was an exciting opportunity.'

Brown had done his research, which relaxed him. He watched numerous Brazil matches back on tape, travelling to see them play in the flesh twice. Bobby Robson was also on hand with advice. 'Most countries had a star player, and it was my philosophy to man-mark and eliminate them,' Brown began explaining. 'But Brazil have numerous star players. I phoned Sir Bobby Robson because he knew Ronaldo from Barcelona and I said to him, "Bobby, how do I handle Ronaldo?" and he said, "You don't!" That was his answer. He said, "I've dealt with some of the best strikers in the world and Ronaldo is by far the best. So, you're wasting your time man-marking him because he'll roll the marker easily." I said, "What about the man behind him?" and he said, "He'll go past him as well." Bobby Robson had said, "You cannot stop him. From a standing position he is lightning fast." He said, "Take a look at Brazil and analyse where he gets his supply, who gives him the ball the most and when you've done that, eliminate the supply." We discovered that he received most of his passes from Cafu, the right-back. So, our job in the opening game was to make sure Cafu didn't play the ball up to Ronaldo. Christian Dailly was the man, an intelligent player, tasked to do it.' Dunga, who liked to get on the ball and dominate play, was another player Brown was keen to stop. Scotland lined up in a 3-5-2 formation with a highly organised zonal defence aided by Champions League winner Paul Lambert offering protection from a deep midfield position.

Both teams were forced to warm up in the changing rooms due to the opening ceremony. Just before the scheduled 5.30pm CET kick-off time, the Brazil team emerged from the tunnel holding hands to form a human chain, a tradition that originated in the USA 1994 qualifiers as a symbol of unity. Comically, Brown tried to use this to inspire his players. 'I shut the door and said, "Look guys, I've just seen the Brazilian team and they're shitting themselves; they're holding hands." The boys laughed at me, but it relaxed them a little and it became a bit of a joke. You do everything possible to get your players in the right frame of mind, relaxed, and not nervous about playing the names on the back of the famous gold jerseys. There was no inferiority complex. They were world champions, but they weren't perfect.'

The afternoon sun cast large shadows across the pitch. In the stands, the excitable Tartan Army and Brazil's yellow-bedecked fans provided the colour, creating a spectacle that wouldn't have looked or sounded out of place at Rio's Carnaval. After just five minutes the pre-tournament favourites took the lead, César Sampaio reacting quickest to Bebeto's corner to head past Jim Leighton. The highlight for Ronaldo was a run during which he mesmerised three defenders before firing at Leighton from a tight angle. The goalkeeper made a save and the ball was bundled away for a corner. At this stage, Brown's best-laid plans looked futile. Then Sampaio went from hero to villain in the 38th minute, giving away a penalty – albeit a soft one awarded by José María García-Aranda. John Collins converted. In the 74th minute, however, a typically adventurous Cafu run was rewarded when his shot hit Leighton, before bouncing into the net via the unfortunate Tom Boyd. Colin Hendry tried to clear the ball off the line but was too late.

It wasn't a vintage display, but the reigning champions were off to a winning start. 'He [Ronaldo] didn't have a great game by his standards because he wasn't getting the ball, the supply was cut off,' said Brown. 'We weren't happy we lost the game, but we deserve credit for the way we handled him – the best player in the world at the time. If I hadn't phoned Bobby Robson I would have man marked him. I wouldn't have put Hendry on him, but I might have pulled Lambert back to mark him.'

With the toughest challenge, on paper, out of the way, Brown felt Scotland still had a chance to progress. However, a draw with Norway and a 3-0 defeat to Morocco, one which Brown feels was closer than the score suggests, meant the Scots finished on one point and exited the tournament after finishing bottom of the group. Brown nevertheless looks back proudly on the experience, 'The ultimate accolade in a career is managing your national team in a World Cup, and to do it in the opening game which is seen in over 100 countries. It's one of the highest-profile games Scotland has played.'

After the Scotland game, Pelé questioned Ronaldo's performance. 'We were hoping he would show the world the quality that we know he has,' *O Rei* said. 'The criticism is normal, so is the pressure,' responded Ronaldo. 'We are here to score goals. And if we don't, we'll be criticised. But I'm relaxed. I've always scored goals throughout my career. I'm not going to stop now just because I'm at the World Cup.'

* * *

Six days later, Brazil faced African champions Morocco, who drew 2-2 with Norway in their opening fixture, in Nantes. Leonardo replaced Giovanni in Zagallo's starting XI and had an early goal ruled out for offside. Ronaldo, whose shorts were already ripped following a confrontation with an overzealous Moroccan defender, opened the scoring after nine minutes. An excellent first-time pass from Rivaldo over the North Africans' defence sat up perfectly for Ronaldo, who had to quickly adjust his feet, to half volley the ball past Driss Benzekri from the edge of the box. Ronaldo looked delighted to open his World Cup account, running to celebrate with the staff and substitutes on the bench. 'My first goal in a World Cup, which I had dreamed of playing my entire life,' Ronaldo said in the 2022 documentary *The Phenomenon*. 'It takes that weight off. Goals have this power; they give strikers confidence.'

Ronaldo cheekily lifted the ball over the head of Saïd Chiba, who showed his disdain by sinking his studs into the forward's left thigh. Remarkably, referee Nikolai Levnikov kept his cards in his pocket. The two players had encountered each other before. When Ronaldo scored his wonder goal for Barcelona against Compostela in October 1996, Chiba was one of the opposition players trying, but ultimately failing, to halt the juggernaut. Before half-time, the imperious Rivaldo doubled Brazil's lead. Five minutes into the second half the comfortable victory was ensured when Bebeto – the 34-year-old veteran and key figure from the 1994 World Cup – made it 3-0. Ronaldo dispossessed Abdelilah Saber on Brazil's left, before leaving another defender for dead with a rapid step-over, poking the ball across for his strike partner to finish from close range.

* * *

Brazil and Norway had to wait a week to face each other in the final game. Not only was the 1998 World Cup the first since the expansion from 24 to 32 teams, but it was also the longest – at 32 days – to date. The Scandinavians had disappointingly drawn both of their matches, leaving them with the unenviable task of having to beat the world champions to progress.

Before the World Cup, Henning Berg had been confident. 'We felt good because we had a team with many players from good clubs in Europe and England, and we felt that we had a team that could compete and go far,' said the Manchester United defender. 'We thought maybe if everything went well, we could do what Sweden did in 1994 and they got the bronze medal. We were ambitious and confident in our ability but of course, in terms of World Cup history it was only the third time Norway had qualified so it wasn't exactly something we were used to.' However, Berg was under no illusions with the task at hand. 'We needed to beat Brazil to go through,' he said, laughing at the prospect, knowing the *Seleção* hadn't lost a group-stage game since 1966. 'It was for sure the most difficult game we could play at the World Cup.'

The Norwegians drew strength from a recent encounter with the world champions but remained wary. 'We had some confidence because the year before we played them in a friendly in Oslo and we beat them 4-2,' began Berg, who had partnered United team-mate Ronny Johnsen in central defence that night. 'Ronaldo and Romário were their strikers that day. We had many fights and many duels. We took an early lead, so they pushed and for most of the game they were chasing us and putting us under pressure and trying to do everything to win the game. With the mobility, quality and skill that these two guys had together, for me as a central defender it was the highest level I've ever played against two strikers. I played alongside Ronny, but we needed the whole team to stop them. That game was a little more open, maybe because it was a friendly, we could take more chances, so we ended up many times one against one, two against two, against these players. We couldn't do that too many times, but we got away with it on that occasion. That game gave us a lot of confidence even though now it was the World Cup, a different category, but we'd played against these players before and we'd won before so that helped us a lot to give us belief but for sure we still did not expect to beat them. We knew that Brazil wanted revenge and wanted to win even though they were through from the group.'

In Marseille's Stade Vélodrome, Egil Olsen selected Berg at right-back, with Dan Eggen partnering Johnsen at the heart of the Norwegian defence. Given that they had already qualified, Zagallo made a couple of changes, but it was still a strong line-up. After 78 minutes, superb work by Denílson on the left was finished off with a diving header from Bebeto. Then the Norwegians hit back with two goals in five minutes. First Chelsea's tall forward Tore André Flo outwitted Júnior Baiano before finishing, then Kjetil Rekdal slammed a penalty past Taffarel to win the match. It was an historic victory for the Norwegians.

Berg faced Ronaldo again in March 1999, as Manchester United knocked Inter out of the Champions League. It meant that he ended his career unbeaten in three encounters with the Brazilian. 'I would not be stupid enough to say I would have liked to have played him every week,' laughed Berg. 'But maybe I would have been a much better player playing against him every week because you have to improve when you come up against these players.'

The Norwegian defender is full of admiration for Ronaldo. 'He's got good movement, he's explosive and links up well. If you're not focused and concentrated and if you don't play together as a team, if you have too many gaps between the lines then he will punish you. You can limit the supply line to him but at his best, he could receive the ball in any position. He could pick up space between the lines, he could make runs in behind you, he can be good for crosses, and he can shoot from 25 yards. To completely stop the supply to him is very difficult and at his best he was very difficult to stop.

'I remember Ronaldo from when he played for PSV and Barcelona, he was unbelievable. He looked like he was playing at a different speed to everyone else. He was on a different level. For me to play against him was something special. His step-overs, the speed, the mobility he had. I don't know if he was the first modern-type striker who could do everything, not only just score goals. He could dribble, shoot, and run past people. I think he's maybe one of the first who did everything.'

For Berg, it was the unpredictability of the likes of Ronaldo and Romário that set them apart, 'They had this top level. Thierry Henry, Alan Shearer, there are so many top strikers at the highest level, but you knew what they wanted to do. The question was could you stop them? With Ronaldo and Romário you never knew what they wanted to do, because they could do so many different things and it was so difficult to read them. For me, that was what made them so good.' Despite their memorable win, a Christian Vieri goal sent the Norwegians packing after their last-16 encounter with Italy.

Two decades later, in June 2018, Brazil and Norway met once again. 'We played Brazil on the 20th anniversary of when we played them in the World Cup,' Berg recalled. 'Ronaldo came with the team, but he could not play. He managed the team. That was good. My kids were very happy because they were able to have some pictures with him.' In front of 15,000 spectators at the Ullevaal Stadion, a match instigated by *Aftenposten*, Norway's largest newspaper, ended in a 3-0 victory to the Brazilians, whose side featured the likes of Rivaldo and Zé Roberto. Kjetil Rekdal, the Flo brothers, Erik Mykland, Ståle Solbakken and company couldn't repeat the heroics of Marseille in the summer of 1998, but fond memories remain for Berg.

* * *

The *Seleção* faced a South American derby in the Parc des Princes in the last 16, against a Chile side that boasted the fearsome front two of Marcelo Salas and Ronaldo's club colleague Iván Zamorano. César Sampaio made it 1-0 for Brazil after 11 mins, heading in a viciously in-swinging Dunga free kick. The defensive midfielder doubled the lead after 26 minutes. A fiercely struck Roberto Carlos set piece hit the wall and ricocheted to the feet of Sampaio, who calmly slotted past Nelson Tapia. In first-half injury time, Tapia brought Ronaldo down as the dangerous forward was attempting to go around him. Ronaldo stepped up to take the kick himself, side-footing the ball to Tapia's left. The goalkeeper got a palm to it but his connection wasn't strong enough to stop a goal. Lazio forward Salas pulled one back after 70 minutes but moments later Ronaldo – who also hit the woodwork twice – got his second. Denílson fed him and he patiently waited for Tapia to make the first move, finishing across the goalkeeper into the far corner the moment he flinched. Inter chairman Massimo Moratti was in the crowd in Paris and afterwards, Ronaldo handed him his shirt as a thank-you for coming to watch.

On 3 July Brazil and Denmark shared five goals in Nantes. The Scandinavians, who beat Nigeria 4-1 in the last 16 to reach the quarter-final, took an early lead through Martin Jørgensen. After ten minutes Ronaldo assisted Bebeto with a lovely reverse pass, the diminutive forward beating Peter Schmeichel via the upright. Ronaldo was the provider once again in the 25th minute, feeding Rivaldo to make it 2-1. In the 39th minute, he spurned the chance to get himself on the scoresheet, heading wide. Brian Laudrup levelled the scores, but a stunning Rivaldo strike on the hour sent Brazil to the semi-finals. While such matches are joyous for neutrals, they are often anathema for coaches. Zagallo had looked unusually animated in the technical area, shouting and gesticulating. Brazil had yet to catch fire and there were question marks over his tactics. Still, he'd led his side to the final four and would ultimately be judged on the black and white metric of winning or losing the trophy.

Three days later, Zagallo took his men back to Marseille for the semi-final to face the Netherlands, who had dumped Argentina out in the previous round thanks in no small part to a breathtaking Dennis Bergkamp effort. It was arguably the first elite opponent Brazil had faced so far. The business end of the tournament had arrived.

At the end of a cagey first half, Ronaldo sprang into action. From a standing start he went from zero to 60 in milliseconds, darting between Phillip Cocu and captain Frank de Boer as Rivaldo sent a pinpoint pass in his direction. Showing exceptional strength and balance to hold off Cocu – who had a handful of Ronaldo's shorts – the striker composed himself before finishing with his left foot through Edwin van der Sar's legs. However, with three minutes of the 90 remaining, Patrick Kluivert equalised with a powerful header. Ronaldo had an acrobatic overhead effort cleared off the line by Frank de Boer in the first period of extra time.

In the penalty shoot-out, Ronaldo stepped up first for Brazil, successfully converting past Van der Sar. Rivaldo and Emerson did likewise; Frank de Boer and Bergkamp scored for the

Netherlands. Cocu missed, handing Dunga the chance to put Brazil firmly in the driving seat, which he did emphatically. At 4-2, Ronald de Boer had to score to keep his nation's hopes alive; Taffarel dived low to his right to save the kick. The goalkeeper became Brazil's hero, mobbed by players and coaching staff alike. The world champions were heading back to the Stade de France, where the tournament began, to defend their trophy.

* * *

Chris Terry, a reporter for Sky Sports in the 1990s, was one of the team tasked with covering the tournament for the broadcaster. 'Those were the days when Sky Sports reporters didn't have any accreditation, we had to do everything by hook or by crook,' Terry began. 'In the lead-up to the tournament, I did an investigative piece into black-market tickets in Marseille which was great fun. For the tournament itself, I was there for the whole time, based in Paris but travelling all over the country.'

Although he covered other teams, Terry's focus was Brazil. 'I did a lot of their training sessions, I worked up a good relationship with the only English speaker, Leonardo, a very charming and courteous man. It was a great scrum trying to get post-training soundbites and interviews because there were hundreds of reporting crews there. You had to elbow your way to the front of this vast crowd and shout as they came off the training pitch. If you were lucky, you got heard and if you were even luckier, they came over and had a chat. Ronaldo was effectively shielded from the media because he was the big star. He didn't seem to do very much media.

'I was astonished at the crowds that came to see them train, crowds that would not disgrace a lower-league football match, they were that box office,' recalled Terry who remembers that the training sessions tended to be focused on skill, and small-sided games. 'They trained in a rather nice, leafy, suburb in the south of Paris, at a nice open lower-league ground with a proper stand. I remember the crowds, there was always a carnival atmosphere, there was often a band playing; it was all very upbeat.'

Throughout the tournament, question marks over Ronaldo's fitness persisted. Two days after the Scotland game he had been seen with an ice pack on his left knee, and rumours of painkilling injections followed the Morocco game. It was admitted before the Denmark quarter-final that his knee problem was preventing him from training properly. Looking back on pre-match photos, with the benefit of hindsight, it does appear that he was not able to fully kneel.

'My impression was that he wasn't the most energetic of trainers, so therefore when he wasn't taking part in the main training session before the final, but instead walking round the touchline with one of the team staff, it wasn't altogether a surprise,' said Terry. 'However, this was the last session before the final and he wasn't out on the pitch taking part. So, I asked around – which was a bit difficult as my Brazilian-Portuguese is non-existent – and they said he'd received a knock, but he was all right, and they were just making sure he was OK and not wanting him to get into any tangles before the final. They very much played down the fact he was not training.

'We got shots of him walking round the outside of the training pitch. The crux of my report was, here was this guy who is the star of Brazilian football and one of the biggest stars in the world not training and being careful about some kind of injury. It suddenly went dark with the question marks over Ronaldo. Looking back, the change of mood in that week and on the final training date was remarkable given what it had been like before, with a joyful swagger in how they went about their business. Suddenly it was overshadowed. They tried to downplay it but there was no mistaking the mood had shifted.'

The night before the final, Dr Joaquim de Mata performed a physiotherapy session on the troublesome left knee.

* * *

What happened to Ronaldo in the hours leading up to the final has arguably become a story bigger than the tournament itself, blowing any concerns over a slight injury out of the water. After waking up at 8.30am local time, he took a walk with room-mate Roberto Carlos. Following lunch, just after midday, Ronaldo retired to room number 290 at the Chateau de Grande Romaine Hotel where the Brazilian delegation was based. At this point everything was normal.

At around 2pm Roberto Carlos went for a lie-down, while Ronaldo went to the bathroom to shave his head. 'The last thing I remember was going to bed,' he told *FourFourTwo* years later. 'After that, I had a convulsion.' Alex Bellos wrote in *The Guardian* in 2002 that, with Edmundo holding him down, César Sampaio was the first person to administer first aid, preventing Ronaldo from swallowing his tongue.

When he came to, he was surrounded by concerned faces. Ronaldo was confused and exhausted by the ordeal. 'I was surrounded by players and the late Dr Lidio Toledo was there. They didn't want to tell me what was going on,' he said. After a walk in the hotel gardens with Leonardo, Ronaldo was told the medical staff had said he was in no fit state to play football, let alone a match with so much at stake. Ronaldo argued, desperate to prove that there was nothing wrong with him. Sometime between four and five in the afternoon they were smuggled out of the hotel's service entrance, setting off for the Clinique Paris Lilas, a designated facility with 24-hour access for World Cup stars. Typically a 50-minute journey, traffic in the French capital meant it took longer than expected. A police escort was required to complete the last leg in quick time. While Ronaldo was preparing for medical tests, his team-mates boarded a bus bound for the Stade de France. Usually the players would be stood up in the aisle, banging drums, dancing, singing, and jovial. Not this time. The camp was sombre, not the buoyant and chest-thumping atmosphere you'd expect before the biggest match of their lives.

After one and a half hours of vigorous testing, the results were inconclusive. The clinic passed on their findings to the CBF officials accompanying Ronaldo, stating that, in their expert medical opinion, he was physically fit to play. Naturally, he eagerly agreed. 'All the essential medical exams didn't show anything was abnormal – it was like nothing had happened,' Ronaldo told *FourFourTwo*. At 7.40pm, just 80 minutes before kick-off, the entourage left the clinic and headed for the stadium in good spirits.

With approximately 45 minutes until the referee's first whistle, Ronaldo arrived. The team sheet, with his name omitted and Edmundo in his place, bearing Zagallo's signature, had already been submitted to FIFA officials, at 7.48pm. As the news filtered through to broadcasters and journalists, the shock was palpable. In the days before news spread across the internet in milliseconds, confusion reigned. At this point no one knew what had transpired in room 290 of the Chateau de Grande Romaine. It wasn't long until the French team discovered the news. Some of them thought it was a trick. 'I've never seen anything like this in my career,' said John Motson on the BBC, in his inimitable style. 'The scenes in the commentary box have been absolute mayhem and chaos.'

Chris Terry was present in the stadium that night. 'On the day of the final itself, I wasn't reporting,' began Terry, who at the time of publication was working for ITV News. 'I was there because I wangled my way in, although I was in the press seats and I got the team sheets and everything else, and I saw, God, Ronaldo's name is not there, that's weird. And that caused a huge stir in the press seats, people were grabbing phones and I called the office, and they already knew because my colleagues were on to it. And then this whole farce of another team sheet being issued with his name on it. It was the most bewildering half hour, 45 minutes, the most extraordinary passage of events.'

As the players were stretching and preparing in the changing room, Ronaldo walked in. 'I had test results in my hand – with Dr Toledo giving the green light,' he told *FourFourTwo*. 'I approached Zagallo at the stadium and said, "I'm fine. I'm not feeling anything. Here are the test results, they're fine. I want to play." I didn't give him an alternative. He had no choice and accepted my decision.' Despite his insistence, it's debatable whether Ronaldo was the best person to decide how fit he was for the biggest game in football.

Half an hour before the 9pm CET kick-off, in a huge U-turn, it transpired that Ronaldo *would* play. According to FIFA's rules, it was possible to change a team sheet if a player was injured or taken ill during the warm-up. This wasn't the case with Ronaldo. Brazil didn't have a warm-up because of their chaotic preparations and even if they had, Ronaldo's issue occurred hours before one would have taken place. One player – a volatile man at the best of times hence his nickname, 'The Animal' – was not best pleased about the development as it meant he forfeited his place in the XI. 'In all honesty, I didn't worry about whether Edmundo would be upset, because you win or lose your place in the team on the pitch,' Ronaldo said in the documentary *The Phenomenon*. When the teams emerged from the tunnel, Brazil were once again holding hands. Ronaldo came out last. It may be easy to say with hindsight, but you could see the worry etched on his face like he was carrying the weight of the world on his young shoulders.

* * *

France started the tournament as 8/1 third favourites according to bookmaker William Hill. They were appearing in their first World Cup Final, and their multicultural team gained popularity and momentum as the competition progressed. *Les Bleus* topped their group before knocking out Croatia, Italy and Paraguay, and although they could count on the mercurial Zinedine Zidane, they also had several unlikely heroes along the way. Hosts versus holders; it was a dream final for the competition organisers, watched by a global audience of more than two billion.

In the Stade de France the night of 12 July was supposed to belong to Ronaldo, but instead, it was Zidane who took centre stage. After 27 minutes the Juventus man drifted away from a daydreaming Ronaldo to head in Emmanuel Petit's corner. Five minutes earlier, Ronaldo had gotten the better of Lilian Thuram on the left wing before whipping in a cross that Fabien Barthez ultimately dealt with. Shortly after the opening goal, Ronaldo outpaced Thuram only to be clattered by Barthez. It summed up his evening. Just before half-time, France made it 2-0 with a goal almost identical to the first. Youri Djorkaeff – Ronaldo's Inter colleague who gave him a warm hug during the pre-match handshake – swung a corner in which Zidane headed home. Ronaldo appeared more alert this time, attempting to intercept the cross, but he misjudged the flight of the ball.

Ronaldo showed a handful of flashes in the second half, most notably finding space in the box to blast a shot towards Barthez after 56 minutes. Despite playing the last 20 minutes with ten men after Marcel Desailly's expulsion, France made it 3-0 in the dying embers of the match. Brazil were, by now, too emotionally and physically drained to take advantage of their numerical superiority. Petit raced through to complete the scoring.

The Brazilian boy wonder was a shadow of his usual self, a ghost-like presence on the Stade de France turf. He was anonymous, there in body but not in spirit. Like he was in a trance. A widely circulated image snapped after the match shows a forlorn Ronaldo standing in the centre circle, reluctantly wearing a silver medal. Also draped around his neck were his silver and blue Nike Mercurial boots. The exhausted and devastated player was consoled by his manager. 'I had a duty to my country and I didn't want to miss it,' Ronaldo later told *FourFourTwo*. 'I had my honour and felt that I could play. Obviously, it wasn't one of the best matches in my career, but I was there to fulfil my role. Then I played and maybe I affected the whole team because that convulsion was certainly something very scary. It's not something you see every day.'

At the time, it was Brazil's heaviest World Cup defeat. If it wasn't for hapless French striker Stéphane Guivarc'h, unable to replicate his prolific club form, the score could have been a lot worse. Although Ronaldo's convulsion and Brazil's defeat dominated much of the narrative, France were deserved winners.

Ronaldo received 15 passes in the final, half the average of the other six games in the tournament. This could have been due to his condition but France were also worthy of credit with their display. There is also no tangible way of proving that Brazil would have won even with a 100 per cent fit Ronaldo. Proving that this triumph was far from a fluke, an excellent generation of French players would go on to win Euro 2000.

'I thought France were outstandingly good, and I thought they played Brazil off the park,' said Chris Terry, watching from the press seats. 'A Brazil side that was not properly functioning, with a figurehead who was not all there, against a French side inspired by Zidane. He was an absolute master. The whole French team were superb, inspired by being on home territory and they played brilliantly. The Brazil side didn't live up to their billing. I felt they were oddly demoralised – they simply didn't play like a team.'

Two days after the fateful night in Paris, the squad landed in Brasilia. They met with President Cardoso and toured the city, despite losing. The Brazilian population were desperate to understand the situation and find out what happened. Ronaldo couldn't wait to escape to his native Rio, although perhaps for the first time in his career, he experienced the toxic side of the media who hounded his every move. 'I'm not a fugitive, I'm not a thief,' he said angrily at the time. 'I'm a normal person who wants to live a normal life and go to my mum's house without being followed by ten or 15 journalists. This is no way to live.' Some much-needed rest and recuperation were required.

* * *

Almost immediately, conspiracy theories began to multiply. Edmundo, hardly a neutral bystander, claimed there was interference from Ronaldo and Brazil's primary sponsor. 'Nike's people were there 24 hours a day, as if they were a member of the technical staff,' he said, before cryptically adding, 'It's a huge power. That's all I can say.' A Brazilian newspaper claimed Ronaldo had a nervous breakdown and had been suffering from depression. Another rumour suggested that Ronaldo's fiancee, Susana Werner, who was based in Paris and working for TV Globo, was a problematic distraction. Ronaldo being spotted at Roland Garros watching the French Open, nine days before the Scotland match, receiving a kiss from tennis star Anna Kournikova surely wouldn't have helped his relationship with Werner.

It was also suggested that the convulsion was due to an adverse reaction to a painkiller. Dr Joaquim de Mata, however, said it had been administered orally – rather than a more damaging injection – and, in any case, the medicine used shouldn't have been strong enough to trigger a convulsion. To the contrary, TV Globo claimed they were told by an anonymous team official that Ronaldo was given an injection of cortisone with anaesthetic on the morning of the final. It was claimed in the Brazilian press that the drug entered a vein accidentally. Brazilian newspaper *O Globo* reported that CBF chief Ricardo Teixeira – son-in-law of João Havelange, FIFA's president from 1974 until the summer of 1998 – pulled rank, overriding medical opinion and the decision of the team's manager. 'If there had been interference, I would have resigned,' Zagallo said. 'I have never accepted interference as coach of any club or national team.' Yet Teixeira himself contradicted this, claiming he had played a role in the squad selection for the tournament, 'To allow the president to make suggestions is part of the routine in any company.'

Other ludicrous insinuations were that Ronaldo was poisoned by French chefs, involved in a match-fixing scam and that the Brazilian and French governments had conspired to allow *Les Bleus* to win the tournament. What's more plausible – and seems to be a common consensus – is that Ronaldo was exhausted and under intense psychological pressure. There were huge expectations on Brazil to win their fifth World Cup, and the best player in the world was meant to deliver. It had been his dream since he was a boy, painting the kerb stones in Bento Ribeiro, and the emotional, rather than physical, stress was the root cause. What complicates the matter is that he had played many important games before, and many after, and another convulsion was never forthcoming. And throughout his career, he was legendary for his relaxed nature before matches. The events of 12 July 1998 will for ever remain shrouded in mystery, an eternal fertile breeding ground for gossip and intrigue.

On 28 July, Zagallo and his staff were fired. In Brazil, coming second is not a consolation. There is winning and there is nothing else. Despite their pre-tournament tag as favourites, Zagallo's side never clicked, were far too cautious, and over-reliant on their star player. Alleged rifts in the camp were exposed by the Ronaldo debacle, which would have shaken any dressing room. Zagallo received criticism for playing Ronaldo in the final but had he stuck with the selection of Edmundo, and lost, he would have been lambasted for that as well. It was a no-win situation that no coaching course can prepare a manager for.

Zagallo was no stranger to the World Cup, winning the tournament in 1958 and 1962 as a player. As a manager he led Brazil to glory in 1970 and was Carlos Alberto Parreira's assistant in the USA as Brazil won their fourth 24 years later. In some capacity, every time Brazil triumphed at a World Cup, he was involved and he had been expected to make it five in France. Seen as the CBF's continuity man, however, his appointment in December 1994 hadn't been universally popular. He was deemed to have failed with Brazil in 1974 and hadn't managed since an underwhelming spell with Vasco da Gama ended in 1991. He was experienced, but there had been younger, more progressive candidates. By 1998 he was already being pilloried for the Nigeria debacle at the Olympics two years previously. He'd tinkered with line-ups and formations and discarded as many players as he had brought back in from the cold. It was a revolving door. He was ultimately replaced by Corinthians manager Vanderlei Luxemburgo a month after his sacking.

After two exhilarating years at club level, and a meteoric rise, the next phase of Ronaldo's career would not be so great. He might have hoped that a return to Milan, and club football, would provide solace. His problems were just beginning.

Chapter 7

Pazza Inter Amala

RONALDO'S DEBUT season with Inter promised so much and hinted at further glory. 'There was huge optimism about what they could go on to do,' said club content man Richard Hall. 'Optimism was heightened, but it's always the same with Inter; they go into every season thinking something special will happen. Inter in those days always thought they would do something, and you never knew.'

Inter's fans were moved by the plight of their star player following his World Cup exploits but Brazil's defeat by France was somewhat irrelevant. 'They were more concerned with how he would come back, and how it would affect his club form,' said Hall. Ronaldo said he was refreshed and ready to go after his summer holiday.

In the summer of 1998, Inter's highest-profile acquisition was Roberto Baggio. Although past his peak, the Divine Ponytail had recently performed remarkably for modest Bologna. Having previously played for Juventus and AC Milan, Baggio had now represented Italy's three biggest clubs.

Baggio could sympathise with Ronaldo when it came to World Cup Final heartache. Just four years earlier, in the searing heat of Pasadena, Baggio – bandaged up and nursing a thigh injury – blazed a penalty over the bar to hand Brazil the title. Ironically, his misfortune gave a young Ronaldo – sitting on the bench and watching events unfold as a raw teenager – a World Cup winners' medal. Following the game Baggio, like Ronaldo four years later, was fiercely under the media microscope.

Baggio's arrival also led to a series of squad number swaps. The newcomer took Ronaldo's vacated number ten shirt after the Brazilian had relieved Zamorano of number nine. The Chilean was given 18. However, bizarrely, a small + symbol was placed between the numbers. One plus eight equals nine. It was a compromise to keep the trio of star forwards happy and perhaps also a small, tongue-in-cheek protest from Zamorano. It also placated the club's new shirt manufacturer – Nike. The Umbro deal had expired and now the American company had almost total control over Ronaldo.

The new season started well enough, with Luigi Simoni's charges picking up ten points from the first 12. In a 1-0 home win over Piacenza, Ronaldo scored a 66th-minute penalty and later that evening he and Brazilian midfielder Zé Elias held a joint birthday celebration. Three defeats in a row followed. In the latter, a 3-2 reverse at home to Bari, Ronaldo netted another spot-kick.

His first goal of the season from open play came on 8 November in the Milan derby. After just seven minutes, Zamorano picked up the ball, with Ronaldo on the outside of Thomas Helveg. In one movement the Brazilian sneaked on the Dane's blindside, picking up the ball between him and Bruno N'Gotty. One touch and a toe-poke past Sebastiano Rossi later and it was 1-0. It all happened in the blink of an eye. It was Ronaldo at his blistering best. However, in what might have been a sign of things to come, he was replaced by Youri Djorkaeff at half-time and the match ended 2-2.

Inter won two of the next three league games. They had qualified for the last eight of the Coppa Italia and were just one win away from winning their group and reaching the same stage of the Champions League. Then, on 30 November, Simoni was fired on the same day that he was awarded the Panchina d'Oro award as the coach of the year. It was a move the club's owner would regret. 'I thought we had a very strong team,' Massimo Moratti later said, 'which, in my opinion, wasn't playing well enough, but I underrated Simoni's importance, and, in fact, the season was a nightmare after his sacking. The regret does remain by wondering what would have happened if he had remained, but I am convinced we would have achieved great things together, as well as less controversy within the club. It was a genuine mistake to send him away, but I continue to admire Simoni, as he never made me feel embarrassed about it. There is great reciprocal respect.'

Simoni's replacement, Mircea Lucescu, had won plenty of honours in his native Romania and, earlier in the decade, had also won promotion from Serie B with Brescia as well as lifting the Anglo-Italian Cup. Seven points from nine was a solid start for the new boss going into the winter break. Ronaldo scored a late penalty in a 1-0 win at Udinese, however Lucescu's side garnered just 12 points in the first three months of the new year, losing six games in the process. That run included a 6-2 victory over Venezia in which Ronaldo scored twice, one of them from the spot. A 4-0 defeat at struggling Sampdoria on 21 March was the nail in Lucescu's coffin. He'd won just four games in 17.

This followed the Coppa Italia exit and just days after Inter had been dumped out of the Champions League by Manchester

United. Much to the delight of manager Alex Ferguson, Ronaldo missed the first leg at Old Trafford. 'The young Brazilian had been on my mind for weeks,' he wrote in his 1999 autobiography, *Managing My Life*. 'At his best, he could destroy any defenders in the world and I had to try and prevent our lads from becoming overawed by the thought of what he might do to them.' Without him, Inter fell to a 2-0 defeat in Manchester – a game perhaps best remembered for the reunion of David Beckham and Diego Simeone, following the Englishman's red card in the World Cup the previous summer.

Knowing he was on borrowed time, Lucescu had rolled the dice in the second leg, selecting Ronaldo as Inter looked to overturn United's two-goal lead. 'The news that Ronaldo was a starter dictated my tactics, I deployed Ronny Johnsen alongside Roy Keane in centre midfield so that either one could choke the space in which the great Brazilian likes to operate,' wrote Ferguson. 'We had an advantage before a ball was kicked. Ronaldo may have been in the blue and black stripes of Inter but not all of him was there … I glanced across to the far corner of the hall and there stood Ronaldo, leaning back with a football pressed between him and the wall. He looked vacant, utterly disinterested in the happenings around him, as if he didn't want to be in that place at that time.'

Henning Berg partnered Jaap Stam at the heart of United's defence. 'He played with Zamorano who was lively and good in the box,' said Berg. 'Ronaldo played but he was not at his sharpest, at his best, even though, again, if you gave him a metre he would hurt you, he would create a chance on goal because he had this quality so for sure if you're not focused, concentrated and right on him all the time then he will give you big problems.'

Ronaldo was replaced on the hour by Nicola Ventola who scored within minutes. However, the visitors equalised on the night with minutes to spare and Inter were out, losing 3-1 on aggregate. Ronaldo's solitary European goal that season came in a 2-1 home win over Spartak Moscow in the group stage.

Lucescu's story was intertwined with that of Marcello Lippi, who had quit Juventus six weeks earlier. With the Romanian still in charge, it was announced that Lippi would take over at Inter in the summer. 'I resigned, I was not sacked,' said Lucescu. 'The biggest mistake was that Lippi's arrival for the following season had already been announced and it was as if I had been destabilised in the eyes of the team. I could only leave.' Lucescu was only ever an interim manager, but it was clear that the looming spectre of Lippi affected his performance and standing within the team.

Goalkeeper coach Luciano Castellini was placed in charge until the end of the season but, of course, it didn't take Nostradamus to predict he wouldn't finish the campaign. His reign started well enough with a 2-0 win over Fiorentina at the San Siro settled by two Ronaldo penalties. Two defeats bookended a 1-1 draw at home to Vicenza which also featured a Ronaldo spot-kick. Just like that, after four games, Castellini was no longer the manager.

The fourth man to occupy the dugout in a whirlwind 1998/99 season was Roy Hodgson, who was Simoni's predecessor and therefore well known to Inter. The Englishman left the San Siro after his contract expired in 1997, joining Blackburn Rovers, but was sacked by the Lancashire outfit the following November. He had since returned to Inter as a technical director having maintained a good relationship with Moratti.

Hodgson's first game of his latest reign was an incredible nine-goal thriller at the Stadio Olimpico. Going into the match, Inter had won just one in ten; Roma, on the other hand, were unbeaten in five of the last six. The home advantage and form guide were with the *Giallorossi*. Latching on to a Baggio pass, Ronaldo gave the visitors the lead after 15 minutes and at the half-time break Inter were 3-1 up. Within minutes of the restart Roma had pegged Inter back to 3-3, then Ronaldo – wearing the captain's armband – made it four. Roma equalised once again then Diego Simeone grabbed a dramatic late winner in an unforgettable match.

Four days earlier Ronaldo had returned to the Camp Nou, representing Brazil in a 2-2 draw with Barcelona to celebrate the Catalan club's centenary. The forward scored the game's opening goal and despite the rain, and his defection to Inter, the crowd applauded their former hero. Time had healed some wounds.

Ronaldo scored in each of Inter's final three matches – two from open play, one from the spot – but they won one and lost the other two. They finished eighth, a massive eight points behind seventh-placed Juventus. Beaten semi-finalists in the Coppa Italia, the *Nerazzurri* and Bologna were paired in a play-off to determine the final UEFA Cup spot for the following season. Bologna won both legs 2-1 and Inter missed out on European football altogether. Hodgson left his role, heading to Switzerland to join Zürich's Grasshoppers.

Ronaldo's total tally was 15 goals – several of which came from the penalty spot – and it spoke volumes about the club's disastrous season that he was their top scorer. He only played in approximately half of Inter's games; the degeneration of the tendons in both knees came to the fore in early 1999, and a carefully managed schedule was deemed a preferable route as opposed to surgery.

* * *

As it so often did during Ronaldo's career, international football proved a welcome distraction during the summer of 1999. Brazil started the Copa América, hosted by Paraguay, sensationally, with Ronaldo netting a brace in a 7-0 thrashing of Venezuela. A 2-1 win over Mexico followed, then a Ronaldo penalty – in his third full game in seven days – gave Brazil the points over Chile. Brazil faced eternal rivals Argentina in the last eight. The *Albiceleste* took the lead via a deflected shot, then Rivaldo equalised with a brilliant free kick. Minutes after half-time, Ronaldo drilled in a low shot from 20 yards which proved to be the winner.

A 2-0 defeat of Mexico in the last four set up a final against Uruguay in Asunción. The gulf in experience showed, with Brazil running out 3-0 winners. Rivaldo had already scored twice when he found himself with the ball in the centre circle. With the outside of his magical left foot, he lifted the ball over the top of the Uruguayan defence for Ronaldo to chase. As the ball sat up, Ronaldo smashed a half volley past Fabián Carini from 12 yards. It was Brazil's second straight Copa América title, won with a 100 per cent record over the tournament. The joint-top scorers, Ronaldo and Rivaldo, netted five goals apiece in Paraguay.

* * *

With Lippi officially installed as Inter's manager – the fifth in two years – the club spent big following the poor campaign, most notably acquiring Christian Vieri for a world-record fee, and goalkeeper Angelo Peruzzi from Juventus. With Lippi – who won nine trophies in five years at the Stadio Delle Alpi – in charge, and Ronaldo partnering Vieri in attack, big things were expected by the *Nerazzurri* faithful. Vieri had been desperate to sign the contract, so keen he was to play with the Brazilian. On paper Inter looked unstoppable ahead of the 1999/2000 season.

With Ronaldo watching from the bench, Vieri started his Inter career well, needing just 16 minutes to score on the opening day of the season at home to Hellas Verona. Ronaldo replaced Zamorano just after half-time and was on the pitch as Vieri completed a hat-trick in a 3-0 win. Ronaldo started the next game, a goalless draw away to Roma, although Vieri replaced him after 58 minutes. He missed the 5-1 home win over Parma altogether, as well as a 1-0 away win against Torino.

In the following match, at home to Piacenza, Ronaldo came from the bench to score the winning goal. As he had previously done at Juve, Lippi loved having a stellar line-up of attackers who could provide different options depending on the circumstances. As well as Ronaldo and Vieri, he still had Zamorano, Baggio, and Álvaro Recoba. Lippi also wanted to make the team less reliant on Ronaldo. His plan was working so far, with Inter picking up ten points from the first 12.

Ronaldo was withdrawn after 63 minutes of the defeat away to Venezia before starting the Milan derby the following week, the first time he and Vieri were named together in the starting XI. With fog from fireworks lingering in the air, captain Ronaldo was felled in the box. He stepped up to send Christian Abbiati the wrong way. The forward looked delighted, as did Lippi on the bench. However, joy turned to pain after 31 minutes after Ronaldo was red-carded – for the first time in his career – following an elbow on Roberto Ayala. The referee dismissed him after consulting his linesman and it was the correct decision. Using their one-man advantage, Milan wore their opponents down to score two goals in the last 20 minutes to win the game.

Ronaldo missed a draw with Lazio due to suspension and then played 90 minutes of a 3-0 defeat in Bologna. The following match – at home to Lecce on 21 November 1999 – was, at first glance, an ordinary fixture in the Serie A calendar. Ronaldo started the game and scored his side's fifth from the penalty spot after just 50 minutes. It was shaping up to be a fun afternoon. Ten minutes later, his world was shattered.

It appeared innocuous at first. Just inside Lecce's half, he sprinted in front of an opponent to control a long pass from his defence. With no contact from the opposition, he suddenly stopped in his tracks and, after receiving medical attention, was replaced by Recoba – who completed the 6-0 drubbing. 'He asked to be replaced and walked normally but when I arrived in the locker room and bent his knee I saw that the centre of the tendon was ripped,' Ronaldo's physio Nilton Petrone told *FourFourTwo* in 2018. This was Ronaldo's first major injury.

Ronaldo went under the knife in Paris the following morning, with Professor Gérard Saillant – one of the world's leading orthopaedic surgeons – performing the six-hour operation at the historic Pitié-Salpêtrière Hospital. Saillant, who specialised in the patellar tendon, said Ronaldo's knee couldn't cope with his explosiveness. A partial rupture was repaired.

Five months of rehabilitation, including regular trips to the French capital followed, before Ronaldo was deemed fit enough to return to a football field. 'Around the beginning of April, we started to think that he was training normally,' Petrone continued. 'He had already been released by the doctor who performed the surgery and told he could possibly make his return to the pitch. At the beginning of that month [April 2000] we travelled, with Dr Franco Combi, who was Inter's doctor, to talk to Dr Saillant about the possibility of Ronaldo playing in the final of the Italian Cup against Lazio. We asked him how much time he would be able to play for and he said 15 to 20 minutes.'

Ronaldo returned to Italy feeling no pain, and training as normal. 'I am very confident,' he said at a press conference. 'There have been cases of injuries much worse than mine where players have made full recoveries with no problems. I hope with all my heart, that if not everything, almost everything that had to happen to me has already happened. The bad luck needs to turn somewhere else now.' While Ronaldo was recuperating back in Brazil, he trained at the beach and CBF headquarters. The day before Christmas he completed an important milestone in his personal life, marrying Milene Domingues, who at the time was five months pregnant with his first child. Ronaldo hobbled towards waiting journalists and photographers before wishing everyone a merry Christmas.

Inter had progressed to the Coppa Italia Final having eliminated Bologna, AC Milan and Cagliari along the way. On 12 April 2000 they headed to Rome for the first leg. Six days before the match, Ronaldo and Milene welcomed their son into the world. Ronald was born.

With Inter 2-1 down after 58 minutes, Ronaldo and Zamorano came on in a double substitution as Lippi looked to get his side back in the tie. It was the Brazilian's first time on a football pitch in a seemingly interminable 143 days, and he even debuted some brand-new silver 'R9' boots, especially for the occasion.

However, a mere six minutes later, tragedy struck, undoing all his hard work over the last five months, undoing Saillant's work. Ronaldo chested down a flicked-on header from Zamorano, took three touches then attempted a trademark step-over close to the edge of Lazio's box. As with the injury against Lecce six months earlier, there was no contact from an opposition defender, only this time Ronaldo wasn't lucky enough to walk off the pitch. He collapsed to the turf, clutching his right knee and screaming in agony. Lazio immediately put the ball out of play, sensing the seriousness of the injury and allowing the medical staff to enter the field. Players from both sides looked deeply concerned, rivalry replaced by human decency. Christian Panucci put his hands to his head, as did Lippi on the bench. Simeone, now playing for Lazio, knelt next to the stretcher to offer comfort after hearing something snap and fearing the worst.

'I cried and I screamed in despair,' Ronaldo said on *The Phenomenon*. 'The pain wasn't actually that strong, but the pain in my heart was enormous.' Having used their three changes, Inter played the remaining minutes a man down and the score ended 2-1, but few people cared about the result. The second leg ended 0-0, therefore Lazio won 2-1 on aggregate and went home with the trophy.

Petrone told *FourFourTwo* that Ronaldo's injury was one of the worst ever suffered by a footballer, 'He ripped the kneecap tendon completely. His kneecap actually exploded and it ended up in the middle of his thigh. Right after the surgery his knee was the size of a futsal ball. We had a few moments at the hospital when he was crying because he wanted morphine to stop the intensity of the pain.'

As a young player, Ronaldo once said his biggest fear was being injured. For the second time in five months he was dealing with a major injury, this one more severe than the first. 'I thought the worst,' he said. 'I just thought that was the end. The end of the line.' It was confirmed that he'd completely ruptured the patellar tendon in his right knee. Saillant was distraught for the pain and suffering of one his highest-profile patients, but also for himself: on a professional level, he'd technically failed. He suggested Ronaldo look for another surgeon but the Brazilian stayed loyal, allowing Saillant to operate. Surprisingly, Ronaldo's first visitor was Zinedine Zidane. The Frenchman made the trip spontaneously and as secretly as was physically possible for a high-profile footballer. The silver lining during the recovery period was that Ronaldo was able to spend more time with Milene and Ronald. The absence of football and endless flights was good for his family life.

During physiotherapy sessions, Ronaldo was only able to bend his knee to 95 degrees, when he needed to be closer to 140. With Nike's help, Ronaldo went to Vail, Colorado, a popular ski resort. The purpose of his trip to the United States was not to hit the slopes; it was for an appointment with Dr Richard Steadman, a famous orthopaedic surgeon who saved the career of Alan Shearer and later Ruud van Nistelrooy as well as stars from other sports such as Dan Marino (American football) and Martina Navratilova (tennis) among others. Steadman suggested further surgery.

A terrified Ronaldo went to Paris to see Saillant who advised against further surgery and reassured him he would return to the field. The professor sent him to the Centre Européen de Rééducation du Sportif in Capbreton, close to Biarritz. Ronaldo spent several months there, mainly working with French athletes from a variety of sports. The days were long and torturous, and a player with a reputation for hating training showed a relentless work ethic. His reward was that, eventually, he could bend his knee to more than 135 degrees. 'It wasn't trophies or goals that motivated me,' wrote Ronaldo in an article for the Players'

Tribune. 'I just thought about that *feeling* – that feeling that I can only find on a football pitch with a ball at my feet.'

Inter finished fourth in Serie A in 1999/2000 and after a play-off against Parma they qualified for the preliminary stages of the ever-expanding Champions League. By the start of the following season, however, trouble was brewing at the San Siro. Lippi, already under fire after losing to Helsingborgs in the qualifying round of Europe's premier cup competition, then oversaw a defeat away to Reggina on the opening day of the league campaign. He told the press after the game that his team 'played like spoilt children who think that they are great players and the victories will just arrive'. He continued, 'That is not fair to those who pay them nor to those who go to watch them. If I was the president, I would dismiss the coach and line the players up against a wall and give them all a kick up the backside.'

Moratti took his advice and terminated Lippi's contract. Ronaldo had little sympathy for the coach under whose watch his knee problems accelerated, helped in no small part by gruelling long-distance runs on Mondays, the day after Serie A games. Marco Tardelli replaced Lippi, although it was another lacklustre season which saw Inter finish fifth in the league and fail to pull up any trees in cup competitions.

* * *

While Ronaldo was recuperating, a political storm was brewing in Brazil; conspiracy theories from the 1998 World Cup Final reared their ugly head once again. The contract between Nike and the CBF – a ten-year deal worth $200m signed in 1996 – had been leaked to the press, revealing that the American sports giant had a say in the organisation of five friendly matches per year, which had to include eight first-team regulars in the starting XI.

In Brasilia, then little-known communist congressman Aldo Rebelo entered a petition in the lower house of Congress to examine the Nike-CBF contract, claiming that it violated Brazil's constitution. Eighteen months after Rebelo filed the petition, and after vehement opposition from the CBF, another scandal brought the issue to the forefront when it seemed to have been dying a slow death.

National team coach Vanderlei Luxemburgo had succeeded Mário Zagallo in 1998 but subsequently saw his popularity plummet. A breakup with ex-mistress Renata Alves shone a light on his finances; accusations of impropriety from the tax authorities engulfed the embattled coach. Things went from bad to worse for Luxemburgo after Brazil lost to nine-man Cameroon at the Sydney Olympics, and he was fired. The dominoes began to fall. Within days of Luxemburgo's dismissal, the upper house of Congress launched an investigation of the most serious importance of the state of the game in Brazil. It breathed new life into Rebelo's petition which had fizzled out. Once and for all, he wanted to discover what happened to Ronaldo on the day of the World Cup Final in Paris, and to what extent Nike's tentacles went into the CBF.

In November 2000, Zagallo took the stand at the commission, and the press packed into the building like sardines. 'Was it his [Ronaldo] being chosen that caused Brazil to lose?' said Zagallo, giving his version of events of 12 July 1998. 'Absolutely not,' he opined. 'I think it was the [collective] trauma, created by the atmosphere of what had happened. If you invert the situation, and I didn't put Ronaldo on and then Brazil lost 3-0, then people would say, "Zagallo is stubborn, he had to put him on, [Ronaldo] was the best player in the world."' Zagallo stated that he had asked Ronaldo at half-time if he was OK and the player said yes. The coach also said he'd make the same decisions all over again if he were faced with the same challenging circumstances.

National team physicians Dr Lídio Toledo and Dr Joaquim da Mata also appeared. Toledo's conscience was clear as the French clinic gave Ronaldo the green light to play. 'Imagine if I stopped [Ronaldo] playing and Brazil lost,' he pondered. 'At that moment I'd have to go and live on the North Pole.' Edmundo – who was due to start the final only for a late U-turn – gave evidence. He contradicted Zagallo's story that he only found out about the convulsion later in the afternoon, suggesting that the coach knew almost immediately. One of them was incorrect, which added to the intrigue.

In January 2001 it was the turn of the star witness to be interrogated. The headliner after all the supporting acts. The dessert after a sumptuous banquet. It's what everyone had been waiting for. Rebelo explained the formalities to Ronaldo, who requested a glass of water. When asked about the Zagallo and Edmundo disagreement over what time the coach knew about the convulsion, he responded rather sarcastically, 'I think at that moment there were more important things to know than if Zagallo had gone to see me or not.'

One deputy asked Ronaldo about the marking of Zinedine Zidane, who scored two headers from corners. He wondered what relevance this had to the relationship between Nike and the CBF. He was asked about his contract with Nike. After stating he could not discuss the finer details of the lucrative agreement, he was told he's legally obliged to divulge all. 'I'm not here to defend Nike or the CBF, but I also have my own opinion,' he began, defiantly. 'I'm here to try to clarify things and to give my opinion if need be. The relationship that I have with Nike is a very good one, because it really never demanded anything of me, apart from using its boots during games, which is the least I could do, and, preferably, score a few goals with their boots. That's the only thing that Nike have ever asked me for.'

Another deputy asked Ronaldo why Brazil lost the World Cup. 'Why didn't we win?' Ronaldo contemplated, 'Because we let in three goals … In football – not just in football, but in sport – you win and you lose … Just because we lost are we going to invent a bunch of mysteries, invent a bunch of stuff?' It was an excellent way to shut down a ridiculous line of questioning.

Ronaldo's role in the inquiry was finished, but the saga rumbled on for months, gathering pace and widening its scope to delve into every dark corner of Brazilian football. Upon its conclusion in May 2001 – after 237 hours and 125 witnesses – a 686-page report was produced. They failed to pin any dirt on Nike, unable to prove that Ronaldo was forced to play in the 1998 World Cup Final due to the demands of some evil, commercial, overlord. Rebelo's petition ultimately came to nothing. Like a baking session with numerous ingredients, and a messy kitchen, with no cake to show for it at the end.

In December 2001 the upper house of Congress concluded their investigation, with a mammoth 1,129-page report. It recommended criminal investigations into numerous protagonists, including CBF chief Ricardo Teixeira, but ultimately nothing happened. 'Brazil's football establishment were saved, as usual, by the timidity of the judiciary, the byzantine complexity of the legal system and the brilliance of the national team,' wrote David

Goldblatt in *Futebol Nation*. The rigmarole wouldn't have looked out of place on one of the soap operas so popular in Brazil. A new contract signed between Nike and the CBF in 2006 excluded any mention of friendlies. Lesson learned. The two organisations remain partners to this day.

* * *

In September 2001 – 17 months after he collapsed against Lazio – Ronaldo was ready to don the black-and-blue Inter jersey and return to the field for a competitive game, after minutes in numerous pre-season friendlies. His new manager, renowned disciplinarian Héctor Cúper, introduced the Brazilian after 62 minutes of the UEFA Cup first round first leg on 20 September at home to Romanian side FC Brașov, a welcome gift for Ronaldo with it coming so close to his 25th birthday.

In the *Irish Times*, Paddy Agnew wrote that Ronaldo looked 'slowish, slightly overweight and distinctly ring-rusty', although this was perhaps expected after such a lay-off. 'This is only the beginning, the first step,' said Ronaldo following the game. 'I've got to keep my feet on the ground and proceed gradually. But you can only get fit by playing, there's no getting away from that … The knee is fine, I felt nothing, absolutely nothing, during the game. I repeat, all I need now is to play regularly and I hope to win back my place in the side as soon as possible. Even if I make mistakes, the important thing is to be playing.'

The fact that he was back on a pitch at all, after so many – media pundits and medical experts alike – had written off his career, was remarkable. 'It was sheer agony, it was a very tough period,' Ronaldo told FIFA.com. 'My family, the physios and the doctors encouraged me to persevere, and it was worth it.

Furthermore, I became a father for the first time at that time and this was a really important motivation for me. The birth of my son Ronald gave me the strength that I needed to withstand that endless torture.'

Three days after his comeback, the cautious Cúper left Ronaldo on the bench for the entirety of a 1-0 win away to Torino. He then received more minutes in the second leg against Braşov, with Inter winning 3-0 to seal a 6-0 aggregate scoreline. His return to competitive action garnered positive press but – from Inter's perspective – it also brought unwanted attention from the national team. Luiz Felipe Scolari had been appointed as Brazil's manager in June 2001 with the *Seleção*'s participation in the following summer's World Cup far from assured. After losing two of his first three games – including a defeat against Argentina – desperation levels had been reached, and Ronaldo was on his radar as a potential saviour.

With three games to go in CONMEBOL's marathon qualification schedule and sitting in joint-fourth in the table – with a potential intercontinental play-off looming – Brazil faced Chile in Curitiba and Ronaldo was called up. 'Obviously, I'm unhappy with this call-up because he is following a very specific programme of work in order to get back to the best condition,' an unhappy Cúper remarked. 'I'm worried he will have to interrupt this very important work for a certain period.' Few would expect an Argentine to help Brazil qualify for a World Cup. Luckily for Inter, Ronaldo didn't play a single minute and, if anything, his presence was about boosting his morale and that of his team-mates who recorded a crucial 2-0 win.

* * *

On 4 November, Ronaldo started against Lecce at the San Siro, but limped off after 17 minutes, replaced by compatriot Adriano. Three weeks later he came on in a 2-0 win in Florence, replacing Vieri after 72 minutes. He was an unused sub in a 4-2 win over Atalanta, then in the UEFA Cup third round he played 11 minutes at home to Ipswich Town.

On 9 December Ronaldo scored his first goal in more than two years in a 3-1 win at Brescia. After just 19 minutes he played a one-two with Vieri before poking the ball past Luca Castellazzi from the edge of the box. His delight was palpable, as was that of his team-mates who swamped him in celebration. He was replaced by Mohamed Kallon after 69 minutes. The positive news of his goalscoring return was a welcome tonic for the club, coming days after the passing of long-term vice-chairman Peppino Prisco. Six days later Ronaldo played the full 90 minutes although it wasn't enough to prevent a 2-1 defeat at home to Chievo.

Then, on 19 December, Inter beat Verona at the San Siro. Vieri gave Inter a first-half lead then Ronaldo scored twice in five second-half minutes. The first was a towering header from a hanging Sérgio Conceição cross; the second included a classic Ronaldo move of taking the ball around the goalkeeper. When he was replaced by Kallon after 75 minutes the San Siro chanted his name and gave a standing ovation. It was the second and last time both Vieri and Ronaldo scored in the same match. The duo played together 11 times, for a total of 667 minutes. With them both on the pitch, Inter averaged a goal every 37 minutes. Had they been able to play together more often who knows what success the pair would have brought to Inter.

Two days before Christmas, Ronaldo started in a feisty 3-2 win away to Piacenza. He won the penalty for the first goal but had to come off with a thigh strain and was replaced by Emre Belözoğlu after 67 minutes. It would be his last club action for more than three months as he flew to Rio for the Christmas break.

At the start of February Brazil played a friendly against Saudi Arabia in Riyadh. Ronaldo was selected in the squad although he pulled up in training so ultimately didn't take to the field. In mid-February he was in Rio for Carnaval, a guest of Brazilian beer company Brahma. On 27 March he played 45 minutes for Brazil against Yugoslavia in Fortaleza. During his extended sojourn in Brazil, Ronaldo was examined by the CBF and their medical experts, including Dr José Luiz Runco, who was by now their head medic. Ronaldo's body fat plummeted, and his sprint times reached similar levels to when he was at Barcelona. He was looking good for the World Cup in the summer.

On 4 April Ronaldo, back in action for Inter, replaced Kallon after 70 minutes of the UEFA Cup semi-final first leg. It was his first Inter appearance for 102 days although it couldn't stop Feyenoord winning 1-0 at the San Siro. For the following league game, Ronaldo was an unused substitute; he then started the second leg against the Dutch side but a 2-2 draw at De Kuip meant the Italians were out, with Feyenoord progressing to the final.

Three days later, Inter faced Brescia at the San Siro. Pep Guardiola gave the visitors the lead from the penalty spot before Ronaldo equalised. Pouncing on a loose back-pass, he went round the goalkeeper but his shot hit the post. Luckily it rebounded straight to his feet. Three minutes later, after a direct run from Turkish midfielder Emre, the ball fell to Ronaldo's feet 20 yards out from goal, he lashed it past the goalkeeper. In a rare show of unbridled passion he whipped off his shirt, seemingly shedding years of frustration in the process. He was dragged to the ground and a pile-on ensued. With a handful of games remaining, the Scudetto was still a possibility.

Ronaldo started for Brazil – alongside Rivaldo and Ronaldinho – in Lisbon, playing the first half of a 1-1 draw against Portugal. With the tournament in Japan and South Korea fast approaching, Ronaldo needed to prove his fitness. Minutes with Inter were of paramount importance.

Back in club action, he scored against Chievo to make it 2-1, although an injury-time equaliser for the hosts – after Ronaldo had been replaced by Ventola – seemed to have scuppered Inter's title aspirations. However, a 3-1 home win over Piacenza the following week, a game in which Ronaldo started and scored the third goal, saw Inter lead the Serie A table going into the final round of fixtures. The first Scudetto in 13 years was within reach and Ronaldo was at the forefront of their renaissance.

* * *

With Juventus second and Roma third, there were three teams able to win the title on the final day. Inter took on a Lazio side with nothing to play for, whose major stars will have had one eye on the upcoming World Cup and whose fans would have preferred *Nerazzurri* to win the title over Juventus or Roma. It was all in their hands, or so it seemed. Inter led twice but by half-time the score was 2-2. In the second half, goals by former Inter man Simeone – who looked almost disappointed to score – and Simone Inzaghi gave Lazio the points.

Despite his side needing goals, Ronaldo was replaced by Kallon after 78 minutes. He sat on the bench, sobbing. Perhaps he knew that, having come so close, he would never win the title with Inter. Perhaps he also knew, subconsciously, that his time at the club was coming to an end. Not only had the Serie A title eluded him, but also his place on the plane to the Far East was far from certain. The day after Inter's heartbreak (Juventus had clinched the title), he nervously waited for the World Cup squad announcement.

Chapter 8

A Perfect Redemption

THE 2002 World Cup in South Korea and Japan – the first to be jointly hosted by two countries – was Ronaldo's third finals. Despite not playing a single minute in 1994 he picked up a winners' medal as a teenager; four years later, he was the best player in the world although the final in Paris was overshadowed by his mysterious seizure as the hosts lifted the cup. For many players, a winners' medal at one tournament then a Golden Ball and a silver medal at the following one would represent a pinnacle few could ever hope to reach. For Ronaldo, cut from a different cloth, there was still a World Cup itch to scratch. At one point his presence in the squad for the 2002 tournament – due to his injury issues – was far from guaranteed. Inter's Argentine coach Héctor Cúper was ignoring him and was public enemy number one in Brazil, seen as the man scuppering their World Cup plans.

After 12 games in the marathon CONMEBOL qualifying schedule, Brazil had 21 points with six matches still to go. There a was real danger that they would be the first Brazilian team not to qualify for a World Cup, which would have been an unthinkable disaster. Luiz Felipe Scolari, who had enjoyed recent club success with Palmeiras, was appointed in June 2001, Brazil's fourth manager of the campaign. Defeat away to Uruguay wasn't the best start to his reign, then wins over Paraguay and Chile were offset by losses to Argentina and Bolivia. Victory over Venezuela in November 2001 meant Scolari's men finished third to qualify automatically, although the final table was so close that just four points separated Ecuador in second from Colombia in sixth. Despite progressing to the World Cup, morale was low. Scolari was said to be cold and aggressive with journalists, and his team wasn't exactly playing an exciting brand of football.

On 6 May 2002, at the InterContinental Hotel in Rio, the manager was the centre of attention at a press conference in which he was due to announce his 23-man squad to go to the Far East. Scolari later said that he had been sure of the first 22 names for a while. However, the last slot was still undecided until relatively late in the day. Many expected Romário to get the nod, and it was seen as a straight shoot-out between him and Ronaldo. Scolari made a decision that changed everything, naming the Inter striker as the final piece of his puzzle. Yet more World Cup heartache for Romário.

Brazil's only warm-up game was a morale-boosting 4-0 win over Malaysia in Kuala Lumpur, nine days before their opening finals fixture. Ronaldo scored the first after 52 minutes and was later replaced by Luizão. Still, not many expected Brazil to win the World Cup. Most bookmakers favoured Argentina, France and Italy over the *Seleção*.

As they had done in 1998, Nike released a highly successful advert in March ahead of the World Cup. The *Secret Tournament* featured 24 top stars, split into eight teams of three, facing off in a knockout competition to determine the winner. Ronaldo was once again at the forefront, as were several other Brazilians. However, unlike *Airport 98* it wasn't all about them, perhaps reducing the pressure on Brazil to be the all-encompassing stars, and especially Ronaldo after what transpired in 1998; perhaps it also represented a more globalised football world. In the end, *Os Tornados* – the team featuring Ronaldo, Roberto Carlos and Luís Figo – won the fictitious tournament. The advert cost US$100m; the soundtrack was provided by a remix of 'A Little Less Conversation' by Elvis Presley.

* * *

Brazil opened their campaign in Ulsan on 3 June. Their opponents, Turkey, took the lead in first-half stoppage time through Hasan Şaş. Five minutes after the restart Rivaldo whipped in a dangerous ball from the left, and Ronaldo attacked it in an acrobatic and unorthodox fashion. 'I had butterflies in my stomach, a bit of insecurity,' said Ronaldo later. 'I didn't know if my knee would take it.' It was his first competitive international goal for almost three years, and after 67 minutes he was replaced by Vampeta.

In the 86th minute Luizão went down under pressure from Alpay Özalan. Kim Young-joo awarded a penalty, despite the challenge appearing to have taken place outside the box, as well as brandishing a red card to the Turkish defender. While it was certainly a foul, with the benefit of replays it appears a free kick would have been the correct decision. The Turkish players were incensed but Rivaldo gladly despatched the penalty to give Brazil a 2-1 lead.

The goalscoring hero turned villain minutes later. Believing him to be time-wasting while waiting to take a corner, Hakan Ünsal blasted the ball at Rivaldo from close range, and the South Korean referee reduced Turkey to nine men. Embarrassingly, the

Brazilian wide man clutched his face when the ball struck him close to his right hip. It was a controversial, and far from convincing, victory, but Scolari's men were off and running. Ronaldo was in pain the following day, purely because he hadn't played so many minutes in a long time, but he was confident that if he could come through a test against an aggressive opponent relatively unscathed then that boded well for the rest of the tournament.

* * *

The kit worn by Brazil throughout this World Cup has become a popular classic. It had fascinating design and engineering features and for these aspects of the famous shirt, there was an Englishman to thank. Hailing from the north-east, Craig Buglass graduated from the prestigious Royal College of Art in 1998. He worked for several large brands until 2000 when he was headhunted to work for Nike in a recruitment drive that was part of a concerted wider campaign to make Nike the number-one brand in football.

Buglass was attracted to the idea of working for the underdog. The challenge was to topple, among others, Adidas, and place Nike firmly at the top of the tree. 'When I arrived at Nike the whole mission was to become number one in football,' he began. 'They knew they couldn't rewrite history, because Pelé and Maradona didn't wear Nike boots. But they looked at the best players in the world and the attitude was, "We're going to create history." That resonated through everything we did.'

With an 18-month lead time from the initial design to the creation of the finished article, Buglass and his team of designers got to work almost immediately to be ready in time for the World Cup. The first aspect of the process was the science. 'It was what we called "form follows function"', he explained. 'We knew if we went to the World Cup with a standard polyester shirt they would be soaking within seconds. We wanted to control how much water the products took on and how quickly it evaporated. By spending a lot of time in Japan, we established the shirts needed to be different. We started experimenting with different fabrics. The whole idea was inspired by termite hills, and how air flows through them. It was decided that we needed one mesh layer that would take most of the moisture and an outer layer which had a waterproof coating so that no rain or moisture could get in. We'd done loads of testing, in wind tunnels and various places around Europe to get the right temperatures. It wasn't a fluke that we came up with the two layers, it was all based around insights and talking to players like Ronaldo.'

Once the science was in place, it was time for the design. Inspiration can come to creative people in weird and wonderful ways, and for Buglass it was no different. Living in Amsterdam at the time, the designer was clubbing in the Dutch capital when he was handed a flyer which featured a striking neon colour. It was a lightbulb moment. 'If you look at the Brazil kit it's a real vivid yellow,' he explained. 'Traditionally it's been more of a canary yellow whereas I wanted to design something vivid.' It wasn't just about looking good, however. 'It was all to do with peripheral vision and seeing your team-mates,' continued Buglass. 'The different coloured shards and lines on the shirts – in Brazil's case, green – were put there deliberately so a player running at full speed can see their team-mates out of the corner of their eye.'

* * *

Five days after the victory over Turkey, Brazil faced China in Seogwipo. Roberto Carlos, who had been practising relentlessly with the Adidas Fevernova, the official tournament ball, smashed in a free kick after 15 minutes. Rivaldo doubled the lead 17 minutes later and just before half-time Ronaldo was hauled to the ground by Li Weifeng. Ronaldinho stepped up to convert the penalty. Ten minutes into the second half, smart play from Cafu on the right led to an easy tap-in for Ronaldo for 4-0. China's well-travelled Serbian coach Bora Milutinović – a World Cup veteran at his fifth tournament with a fifth different nation – had no answer to the 'Three Rs' of Rivaldo, Ronaldinho, and Ronaldo, all of whom had scored. The attacking trident was a blessing for Ronaldo, meaning that, unlike in 1998, the burden of pressure to create magical moments was shared. Protecting his star man once again, Scolari brought on Edílson after 72 minutes. Despite two victories out of two, journalists back home remained largely negative, with many questioning the standard of the opponents.

The final group game pitted Brazil against Costa Rica in Suwon, and it took Ronaldo just ten minutes to score from close range after Edílson's cross. The 25-year-old doubled his tally minutes later, showing quick feet as the ball came loose following a corner. A goal for each side meant that the score was 3-1 at the break. Costa Rica pulled another back after 56 minutes before Rivaldo and Júnior – Roberto Carlos's understudy – sealed the victory. Brazil moved to the knockout phase with maximum points. Ronaldo, who completed 90 minutes, now had four goals, as many as he scored at France '98.

In the round of 16, Brazil faced Belgium in Japan. The Red Devils had a goal disallowed by Jamaican referee Peter Prendergast after captain Marc Wilmots was adjudged to have pushed his marker before heading past Marcos in the Brazil goal. Twenty-two minutes into the second half, Rivaldo – who joined AC Milan later in the summer – gave Brazil the lead with a stunning half volley from the edge of the box. In the 87th minute, substitute Kléberson centred from the right and Ronaldo finished first time. The victory over tough opposition gave Brazil confidence going into the last eight.

England awaited. The Three Lions emerged from a tight group in second place, a slender victory over arch rivals Argentina proving decisive. They comfortably beat Denmark 3-0 in the previous round and had trounced Germany 5-1 in Munich in qualifying. England would be a severe test of Brazil's credentials, and Michael Owen pounced on a mistake by Lúcio to give them a 1-0 lead after 23 minutes. Then, with almost the last move of the half, Ronaldinho drove at the English defence before pushing the ball out wide to Rivaldo who swept it past David Seaman and into the far corner with his left foot. As the cliche goes, it was the perfect time to score as it meant the momentum was with Brazil heading into the break.

Five minutes into the second half, Ronaldinho looped a free kick over the head of Seaman and into the top corner from 42 yards. It was either a fluke, mishit cross or a stroke of genius depending on who you talk to. For England's number one, it brought back unfortunate memories of May 1995, when Real Zaragoza's Nayim lobbed him from long range in the dying stages of the Cup Winners' Cup Final, condemning holders Arsenal to a heartbreaking defeat.

England were given a glimmer of hope seven minutes later when Ronaldinho was harshly red-carded by Felipe Ramos, the Paris Saint-Germain forward adjudged to have shown his studs when challenging Danny Mills for the ball. Ronaldo was replaced after 70 minutes and Brazil hung on to progress to the

The sorcerer and the apprentice. Ronaldo celebrates the 1994 World Cup triumph with Romário.

In action for PSV Eindhoven.

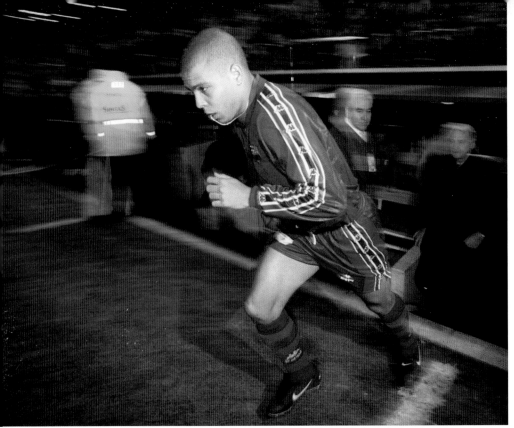

Fast as lightning.

Parading the Cup Winners' Cup with Robson and José Mourinho in Rotterdam.

Ronaldomania hits the San Siro ahead of his Inter debut.

FIFA World Player of the Year, for the second time in a row.

With the UEFA Cup after one of his best performances in an Inter shirt.

Stopping Ronaldo was at the forefront of Craig Brown's mind as Scotland faced Brazil in the opening game of World Cup '98

Scoring an excellent goal against the Netherlands in the semi-final.

Grappling with
Henning Berg
as Inter host
Manchester
United in the
1999 Champions
League quarter-
final second leg.

On the road to
recovery. Working
hard after knee
surgery.

final four. It was the only game during the whole tournament in which he failed to score but the other two members of the fearsome attacking trident stepped up to the plate. England's Rio Ferdinand, one of the best defenders of his generation, summed up facing Brazil in his 2006 autobiography, *Rio: My Story*, 'Ronaldo faced me up on the left-hand side of the box and played it into Rivaldo. Ronaldo then made a run past me to get the one-two and as I turned back to challenge he stepped inside again. I realised at that moment that this game was different from any I'd been in before. No one had ever done that to me.'

The semi-final in Saitama pitted Brazil against group-stage foes Turkey, who had eliminated co-hosts Japan, and Senegal, in the knockout phase. Turkey – competing in just their second World Cup – were still livid following the earlier exploits of Rivaldo, as well as other incidents they felt went against them. A tasty encounter awaited. After sustaining a knock to his left abductor against England, Ronaldo was in a race to be fit with the punishing tournament schedule taking its toll. Turkey weren't expecting him to play and the 'will he, won't he?' debate dominated press coverage in the build-up. After the previous World Cup Final, it was the last thing Ronaldo, or Brazil, needed, so he conjured a hilarious and spontaneous plan to focus the news elsewhere. When shaving his head, as he did as a ritual before every game, Ronaldo decided to leave a triangular patch at the front, much to the amusement of his team-mates. Scolari, who thought it was unprofessional and disrespectful, was not so enamoured. The haircut became a craze with kids across Brazil copying their hero, much to the annoyance of the country's parents. Mischievously, the forward said, 'I can't disappoint all the kids who have copied this style,' and vowed to keep it for the game. Some would say it was weird, but you could also say his decision to do this was thoughtful, genius even.

With Ronaldinho missing through suspension, the semi remained goalless at half-time but four minutes after the teams had returned to the field, Ronaldo scored the only goal of the game after receiving the ball from Gilberto Silva. Unable to kick with the inside of his left foot or his laces due to the pain, he summoned muscle memories from his futsal days, improvising and catching the goalkeeper off guard with a toe-poke before he expected a shot. A rare show of aggression against Turkey showed that Ronaldo, for his usually cheery demeanour, was not a player to be pushed around. It also showed how desperate he was to progress to the final. 'We fell together to the floor and after we both got up he [Turkish defender Bülent Korkmaz] stepped on me then hit me with his fist on my head,' said Ronaldo. 'That made me very angry. That was why I reacted.'

Ronaldo was in floods of tears after the game, having qualified his nation for a third successive World Cup Final. 'I don't feel I have any need to explain the last two years of suffering which I have been through,' he stated. 'But I have to say the nightmare is now over. Every time I take to the pitch, for me it is an honour and a joy, and every goal I score is a victory. Now, in helping Brazil to the final, it is my aim to continue such happiness. It is a final in which I plan to score the most important goal of my career.' Scolari, at one point under fire, was naturally equally delighted, 'It is really something very big what we have achieved but I felt positive energy from the Brazilian players, supporters and the bench. We are pleased that we have now been able to make the fans so happy and we thank them for having the patience.'

Before the final, Scolari showed the players a motivational video. The homesick squad had been away from their families for more than seven weeks, and the video showed the players celebrating, and hugging. Several of them were crying at the film, and when it finished they clapped. There was little mention of Germany in the pre-match briefing; it was a masterstroke. Back home, TV Globo had visited the players' hometowns. They went to Bento Ribeiro where kids had done exactly what Ronaldo did in 1982, almost two decades earlier. Despite the distance, there was a unity between the Brazilian public and the national team that seemed unlikely just weeks before.

On the day of the final, Ronaldo was keen to avoid a repeat of what transpired four years earlier. 'Until the day of the final, I honestly hadn't thought about '98,' he told the 2022 DAZN documentary, *The Phenomenon*. 'But after lunch, the ghost of '98 haunted me a lot. I didn't want to go up to my room for a nap. So, I walked around the hotel corridors to see who was awake ... I didn't tell anyone how I was feeling. After a while I couldn't find anyone to talk to. I was very scared about a repeat of '98 ... Well, I didn't have a seizure.' Other members of the squad had demons to exorcise. 'I don't want to cry again,' said Roberto Carlos.

Yokohama, 30 June. Ronaldo's date with destiny. When a Hollywood-esque story of rise, fall, and redemption was given its pulsating, happy conclusion. Imposing Italian referee Pierluigi Collina oversaw proceedings in front of almost 70,000 spectators. Cafu, appearing in a third successive World Cup Final, captained the *Seleção* against Germany. The two sides had outstanding pedigree; both were appearing in their seventh final, although curiously they had never met at this stage. And since 1938 there had been just one final, the 1978 encounter between Argentina and the Netherlands, not containing either of the powerhouses of international football.

The pre-match photo was slightly unusual, yet it showed the togetherness of the squad that had organically developed during the 53 days they had spent together. Vampeta played in 15 of the 18 qualifiers but had just made one substitute appearance so far at the World Cup. Yet it was his idea that, rather than just the starting XI lining up on the pitch in front of a throng of photographers, all 23 members of the squad should be present. It was a symbolic show of unity.

In the 67th minute Ronaldo made his mark. He wasn't typically used to pressing when out of possession, but it was something Scolari encouraged among his forwards. Ronaldo was dispossessed, falling to the floor. He rose immediately, hunting down Dietmar Hamann and relieving him of possession with a perfectly legal shoulder barge, before taking a touch and passing to Rivaldo. German captain Oliver Kahn – perhaps prematurely named as player of the tournament before the final – committed a rare error, attempting to scoop up Rivaldo's shot but instead spilling the ball into the path of Ronaldo who, like all opportunistic forwards, had gambled, continuing his run into the six-yard box; 1-0.

* * *

The famous boots worn by Ronaldo to open the scoring on the grandest stage of all were designed by a colleague of Craig Buglass. After graduating from studying product design in Manchester, Leeds-born Peter Hudson joined Nike in 1996. Until the spring of 1998 his focus was tennis rather than football. Like Buglass, Hudson was excited at the prospect of helping Nike conquer the final frontier, the remaining major sport the brand was not the global leader in, 'The first Nike product created with a swoosh was a football boot, back in the early '70s. They already knew that they wanted to get after soccer but had tried and failed a couple of times. They later made the strategic decision to commit to authenticating themselves as a global brand which is where I and a bunch of other guys were lucky to come in at a perfect moment.'

Like with the shirts, the process for the boots that Hudson was to create – what became part of the Mercurial Vapor range – would take between 18 and 24 months from start to finish. He explained, 'First of all, we asked ourselves, "What does performance mean, and what is Nike football footwear?" We knew what Adidas stood for: comfort, tradition, leather, black and white colours. We had to determine what our creative strategy was, the innovation perspective, and what could differentiate Nike from the other boots on the market. I flew from Oregon to Europe to spend weeks with professional athletes to figure out what was going on in football, and how the game was connected to not only a matchday but also to culture. The macro strategy I came up with – one half of the coin – was that we had to create a performance perspective to the footwear that was equal to or better than Adidas.'

Leather was a mainstay in most boots until Hudson and Nike's innovative methods introduced carbon fibre and other new materials to the manufacturing process. However, it was heavy, especially when wet. Nike were looking to the future and change was needed for improved performance. Hudson said, 'I realised in my research that football was getting faster, the players were more athletic, and sports science had been introduced. Speed and attacking football meant that boots had to be incredibly light.

I stripped the boots down to the most minimal construction possible, removing the materials that made them heavy. I wanted them to fit like a perfect glove because so many players in the past were injured by wearing boots that didn't fit properly.' Detractors would, inevitably, come. 'Some players were against it and physios worried it would cause metatarsal injuries,' continued Hudson. 'It was just fear of change. The boots had stability where you needed it, and touch where you needed it.' The idea was that players could escape dangerous situations with their lighter boots. Initially designed for the fastest players, invariably the forwards, soon those in all positions wanted them. The likes of Ronaldo, in Nike's top tier, would have boots specifically fitted for their feet, to act almost as a second skin.

With the performance aspect of the boot sorted, the other side of the coin was fashion. 'I was determined that the product could be beautiful. Everyone takes it for granted now that Nike football is highly stylised and colourful, but that wasn't a thing back then. When you bought football boots in the past you bought a black leather piece of equipment,' said Hudson. If the inspiration behind the colour of the shirts came from the Amsterdam nightclub scene, for the boots it was a training ground in the north of England. 'I'd been to a bunch of different clubs, and it was autumn in the late '90s,' he continued. 'It was rainy and cold and the wind was blowing sideways. I was on the training field, and all the players were wearing black boots and dressed in dark clothing. They were covered in mud and looked like drowned rats. I was waiting to meet a couple of players and when they emerged from the changing room it struck me. They were young guys, fit as a fiddle, suited and booted looking all polished, they were holding designer wash bags and getting into their expensive cars. I realised that they wanted cool equipment that matched their fashion. That was my lightbulb moment and I created the strategy that we would have not only the lightest, fastest equipment in the world but also the most beautiful.'

Synthetic materials allowed the designers to be more flexible and creative. Hudson added, 'I created the chrome-coloured Mercurial because under the floodlights and against the flashes of photographers' cameras, there was no colour that was going to do it so I came up with this concept of "anti-colour", reflecting the environment, reflecting colour, reflecting culture, and that's where it came from. Change agents come along and when you shift the paradigm within a culture that is ready for change then things move fast. We opened the dam to what people wanted, which was new lightweight and coloured materials.'

From the beginning, Hudson had faith that Nike would succeed in their mission, having seen first-hand with previous employers Dunlop and Mitre that brands rarely stay at the forefront for ever. 'It depends on who you talk to,' Hudson explained after I asked when the company became the undisputed number one. 'The financial people – who regard winning as making money – would say the late 2000s was the point that they were profiting from football. But for us, it wasn't about that. We wanted to win the hearts and minds of kids who loved football, and of professionals who would see Nike as an authentic supplier of equipment. I think we had reached that point by 2008, which is eight years after starting. That's a blink of an eye in the footwear world, considering Adidas were the world leader for decades.'

The designer, who left Nike in 2016 and still resided in Oregon at the time of publication, was keen to stress the authenticity of him and his colleagues, and how genuine the company's mission was, 'There was a purity to it. They truly believed football could be a positive cultural force around the world, and truly believed that football was a joyous thing.'

Ronaldo's smiling face after scoring a goal proved that more than anything.

* * *

Twelve minutes after Ronaldo opened the scoring in the final, the Brazilians launched another assault on Kahn's goal. On the right, Cafu passed to Kléberson before continuing his run. The midfielder, who later moved to Manchester United, drove into the German half, using his captain as a decoy. Kléberson then centred the ball in the direction of Rivaldo, on the edge of the box, who dummied into the path of Ronaldo. One touch and a pass into the bottom corner later and it was 2-0 to Brazil. Kahn, who conceded one goal in six games en route to the final, keeping six clean sheets, had now conceded twice in the space of 12 minutes. If it wasn't already, Ronaldo's legacy as a legend of the game was set in stone.

In the 90th minute, Scolari withdrew Ronaldo, replacing him with Denílson. Many managers have used this trick before, allowing the star of the show to have an almost intimate moment with the crowd. For Ronaldo, this touch of humanity from the coach would have meant more than it may have to other players. 'When I came off, I started to see the whole movie of my last four years,' Ronaldo told *The Phenomenon*. He'd famously been on the bench before, crying, while playing for Inter, after the Scudetto had slipped through their fingers, but that seemed to be in a past life. These were happy tears. He embraced Ronaldinho, his partner in crime throughout the tournament, another wonderfully gifted talent that helped shift the burden of expectation from Ronaldo's shoulders.

Rodrigo Paiva was another man who shared an emotional embrace with the match-winner. 'When I got to the sideline, I saw Rodrigo Paiva, the press secretary for the national team,' wrote Ronaldo in a 2015 article on the Players' Tribune. 'This man had been with me at every point in my recovery. He used to walk slowly beside me when all I could do was walk. I just lost it and started crying. All of this emotion, I had never felt anything like it before.' When interviewed for *The Phenomenon*, Paiva claimed Ronaldo whispered in his ear, 'God was good to me, wasn't he?'

* * *

Throughout the final, Germany had more shots on target, more corners, and 56 per cent possession, yet the statistic mattering most belonged to Brazil. Cafu, the record-breaker, lifted the famous trophy. The BBC called it the 'World Cup of shocks' and although Brazil weren't cast-iron favourites before the tournament, it could never be classed as a surprise to see a Brazilian raise the biggest prize.

Ronaldo sobbed with unbridled joy after the final whistle. The flag was draped around his neck, then he sat upon Júnior's shoulders. He hugged Rivaldo and then the pair of them waved the flag, surrounded by photographers. The Brazil players, as well as technical staff, formed a huge circle. On their knees, holding hands, they prayed. Pelé handed Ronaldo his medal and both were all smiles, a world of difference from the mood four years earlier.

En route to victory, Brazil conceded just four goals in seven games, belying suggestions they were weak defensively or, on the other hand, showing that attack is indeed the best form of defence. At the other end, Scolari's men scored 18, finding the net in every match. In winning a record fifth World Cup, Brazil had won all seven of their fixtures in normal time, without the need for a penalty shoot-out.

Ronaldo, the man with the chrome Nikes, won the golden boot after scoring eight goals and was also named in the all-star squad. His prolific form meant he moved to third in the all-time World Cup scorers list, joint with Pelé on 12 goals. Only France's Just Fontaine and Germany's Gerd Müller stood in his way. 'I worked for two and a half years to recover from injuries and God reserved this day for me and for the Brazilian national team,' he said. 'I've said before that my big victory was to play football again, to run again and to score goals again. This victory, for our fifth world title, has crowned my recovery and the work of the whole team.' Speaking to *Sports Illustrated* in 2021, Ronaldo said, 'Those two goals represent my big fight for two years.' And reflecting for *The Phenomenon*, he reflected, 'The honest truth is that I had already won my World Cup. My World Cup was my recovery. And going through that difficult period made me a better friend. It made me a better son. It made me a better dad. And it made me a much better person.'

* * *

When Ronaldo's injury situation was at its worst, many people felt he would never return to professional football, let alone become the chief protagonist in the World Cup Final. Many Brazilians initially wanted Romário in the squad over Ronaldo, but the result justified the manager's decision. Scolari worked hard on integrating the team and building a solid bond. At the team hotel the delegation took up an entire floor, with a large common room where they not only ate but also played pool, table tennis, computer consoles and even bingo. There, and on buses to training and matches, there was a fun atmosphere. Scolari was renowned for his man-management and ability to build a unified squad. Even to the time of going to print the players were part of a WhatsApp group chat simply called *Penta* (Fifth), the bonds of success meaning they remain close.

Looking back on their links to Brazil's triumph, Buglass and Hudson have nothing but pride. 'I was crying my heart out, thinking, "Is it ever going to get any better than this?"' said shirt designer, Buglass. 'Football is just one side of what I do but nothing I have touched since that day has ever got anywhere near that level. The legacy I'm going to leave behind gives me an amazing feeling.' Hudson, the creator of the boots that graced Ronaldo's gifted feet, echoed Buglass's sentiments, 'You spend so much time travelling and pouring yourself into the products, with a team, so the validation and the way it was seen on that global stage in front of billions of people: it doesn't get better than that. It's an extension of yourself, it's a validation of your hard work and that of your team, and when you're a creative designer it's not just a product. I believed in my heart and soul, through the research, that this is right and when it gets validated there is nothing like it. When a design connects like that it is incredible and those moments are unforgettable. The boots are burnt into history. It's very humbling.'

The plane ride home from the Far East was a festive affair. Ronaldo sat with his two-year-old son, Ronald. His father was also there. On the approach to Brasilia, four fighter jets from the Brazilian air force accompanied the commercial aircraft on the final leg of its journey. The cockpit windows were opened and

Brazilian flags were proudly thrust into the air. The triumph unified the country in a way that only football can. How a divided Brazil could today do with similar heroes.

Upon arrival in the capital, a red carpet and a welcoming committee was waiting. Half a million people lined the streets. In Tres Poderes Plaza, the squad was greeted by the president. One by one they approached Fernando Henrique Cardoso who presented them with medals to celebrate their honour and merit. Numerous other Brazilian cities were also able to celebrate their heroes who toured the country. From the depths of despair, Ronaldo was now on top of the world. His club career was also about to take a positive turn after four years of hell.

Chapter 9

The Third *Galáctico*

RONALDO'S HEROICS in the Far East made him a natural choice for Real Madrid, his acquisition encapsulating their Florentino Pérez-driven project of adding a star player to the squad each summer. The club president, elected in July 2000, controversially snatched Luís Figo from bitter rivals Barcelona that same month, before signing Zinedine Zidane from Juventus in 2001. Then the best player and top scorer at the 2002 World Cup, Ronaldo, became the third of the so-called *galácticos*. Despite Real having just won their third European Cup in five years, the addition of star power to their ranks showed no signs of slowing down.

It was a miserable four years for Ronaldo between the two World Cups, punctuated by serious injuries and poor relationships with more than one of Inter's many head coaches. The incumbent at the time of his departure, Argentinean Héctor Cúper, was surprisingly backed by Massimo Moratti, a long-time supporter of Ronaldo. 'I loved Inter very much, I was very comfortable in Milan, I had an unconditional love of the whole city, maybe all of Italy, but with the coach we had I couldn't continue,' the Brazilian told DAZN Italy in 2020. 'I spoke with Moratti and said, "President, I cannot continue with this coach. Either you send him home or I go." Unfortunately, on the one hand, because the story with Inter ended there in a very ugly way, he chose Cúper before me.' Ronaldo said Cúper's training sessions were physically damaging to him, making him dread going to work. Cúper didn't believe in treating people fairly, according to their circumstances; he believed in equality. There was no preferential treatment. Ronaldo described him as 'the worst coach I had in my entire career'.

Inter turned down Real Madrid's initial advances, with Moratti negotiating hard. But after Ronaldo had reiterated his desire to leave in a meeting on 28 August, there was little choice but to let him go. Despite the way his time at the San Siro ended, Ronaldo was still left with a heavy heart. 'I wasn't able to train with the other players,' he said. 'Soon after that, I could not leave my house. I could not enjoy the pleasure of being world champion. I could not even say goodbye to people at Inter, my colleagues. I had to listen to people trying to destroy my image. It was easy to attack me and paint me as the villain. Overnight I became the worst person in the world – the anger was incredible, people decided to show no respect. It was out of proportion. I was depicted to Inter fans as someone who did not care for the club, and that is a lie – I cried like a baby when we did not win the league the previous year [2001/02].'

With hindsight, it may seem like a poor decision for Inter to have let him go but at the time – even with the World Cup success behind him – it was obvious Ronaldo needed a change of scenery to reignite his club career. The move may have also benefited the *Nerazzurri*. 'Inter had to be less focused and less dependent upon Ronaldo,' said Ciaran Crilly, long-time season ticket holder and memorabilia collector.

'Moratti thought Cúper was the one to sort the dressing room out, so he backed his man,' said Richard Hall, who works on Inter's official English-language coverage. 'You think about it at the time, it makes sense, it's not the worst decision.' Hall also believes the conditions weren't optimal for Ronaldo to have been a success at Inter. 'To understand Ronaldo's time at the club you have to understand Inter,' he said. 'Inter at the time was unstable. It's so Inter to sign Ronaldo and not win anything. It's typical, perfect Inter. You buy the best player in the world, you don't win anything, and then he gets injured. We bought the best player in the world. He was amazing for a period. But we just didn't think about what went around him, what structure we needed to support him.'

The transfer to the Spanish capital was confirmed on Saturday, 31 August 2002, just three hours before the deadline, for a fee of €45m. It came two months to the day after the Brazilian's two goals sunk the Germans in Yokohama and the day after Real Madrid had lifted the European Super Cup by beating Feyenoord 3-1 in Monaco. Fernando Morientes refused to give up his number nine shirt, so Ronaldo took 11.

As well as escaping Cúper, the lure of Real Madrid was difficult to turn down. 'My dream was to play one day in Madrid and I fought until the last moment to come,' Ronaldo told DAZN Italy. 'I had Roberto Carlos in the team who told me everything that Madrid represented and what he lived in Madrid. That left me curious and after years I wanted to see with my own eyes. I went to Madrid and the truth is that it is much bigger than what Roberto said and what I could imagine.'

Despite the World Cup success, Ronaldo was still a risky purchase for Real because of his injury record. Influential forward

Raúl was unsure it was necessary, given the presence of him along with Morientes, Javier Portillo and Guti who had been performing well in an advanced role. There were question marks about the influence of marketing over the decision to acquire the Brazilian, especially in the club's centenary year. However, little of this was personal, nor did it reflect on Ronaldo as an individual. It was more a case of gripes between the star players and the club hierarchy. Steve McManaman, a Real Madrid player at the time of Ronaldo's arrival, wrote in his 2004 book *El Macca: Four Years at Real Madrid* that, for the most part, the players were 'thrilled'.

Eduardo Álvarez, a Real Madrid supporter and journalist who has written for ESPN and the BBC, was delighted with the acquisition, despite misgivings. 'We thought it was a gamble, but we were cautiously optimistic,' Álvarez began. 'He had just played a very good World Cup and alongside the other *galácticos*, we thought it could work well because he was going to get good service. Even though he wasn't great in the air we knew his team-mates would find him in space. He was a one-man offensive system. With him in the side, you could trust that something was going to happen during the match and that he was going to be in a scoring position regardless of his physical condition. However, we also knew he had suffered a bunch of tough injuries, one of them potentially career-threatening.' For Álvarez, Ronaldo's previous affiliation with arch rivals Barcelona was irrelevant, 'He was amazing at the Camp Nou, unstoppable, but there was nothing negative relating to his Barça connection. There had already been some players – like Bernd Schuster and Figo – that had successfully made the switch. He had a great time in Barcelona, but it was five years earlier.'

THE THIRD GALÁCTICO

Following a successful medical on Monday, 2 September, the same day his new club opened their La Liga campaign with a 2-0 home win over Espanyol, Ronaldo formally signed a four-year contract. In front of a throng of animated journalists, and the flashing and clacking of numerous cameras, he was presented at the Santiago Bernabéu Stadium. 'I hope to fulfil expectations,' he said, a day after arriving at the Torrejón Air Base after the club whisked him from Milan to Madrid in a private jet. 'I know it's a great responsibility. I hope to respond with lots of goals and beautiful moves. I'll try and do all I can to meet the expectations. Thank you.' Then it was time to change into the kit and be paraded on the sun-drenched pitch for the obligatory keepy-uppies.

After gleaning seven points from the first three games without the injured Ronaldo, who had pulled a muscle in training and missed the pre-season programme, an unbeaten Real welcomed Alavés to the imposing Bernabéu on 6 October. Following weeks of speculation and excitement about when Ronaldo would debut for his new club, the day had arrived, with the Brazilian named as a substitute by manager Vicente del Bosque. With the home side 2-1 up, Ronaldo came off the bench 20 minutes into the second half, replacing homegrown striker Portillo. Ronaldo and Portillo were perfect examples of Real's 'Zidanes y Pavones' policy of combining externally acquired megastars such as Figo, Zidane, and Ronaldo, with homegrown, low-maintenance youngsters like Francisco Pavón and Portillo who knew the club inside out and understood the expectations of the fans.

Superstitiously touching the turf before crossing himself three times in rapid succession, Ronaldo's higher power must have been watching as a dream debut unfolded. Controlling a

Roberto Carlos cross with his chest, Ronaldo found himself in space in the penalty area. Given time to allow the ball to bounce, he fired the ball off the grass and into the top corner of Richard Dutruel's goal to make it 3-1. It was an important goal because the visitors were growing in confidence as they searched for the equaliser and it had come less than a minute after his introduction.

A goal from either side made it 4-2 before Ronaldo grabbed his second with ten minutes remaining. Resplendent in the famous all-white kit, the new number 11 slid the ball home after a pass from McManaman, the Liverpudlian who had taken advantage of the Bosman ruling to sign for the club on a free transfer in 1999. The two would strike up a perhaps unlikely friendship, their easygoing personalities allowing them to gel on and off the field. The brace brought the infectious smile back to the 25-year-old's face, and a new era had begun after four difficult years at the San Siro. A late chance even went begging, denying Ronaldo a hat-trick. After scratching his head in frustration, another smile cracked on his face.

Following the match, he said, 'It's better that I didn't get a third, or it would have created too much expectation.' The hype had been building for weeks. Ronaldo was virtually ever-present in the pages of *AS* and *Marca*, influential daily sports newspapers in Spain. In *AS* the following day, Tomas Roncero referred to him as 'God with a child's face'. *Marca* called it 'the mother of all debuts'. Eduardo Álvarez remembers Ronaldo's first appearance vividly, 'When he walked on to the pitch, I first thought he was completely out of shape and perhaps shouldn't be playing. Especially given his knee problems; you don't want to be overweight when you have knee injuries. Yet he scored within minutes of joining the match. He had scored within a couple of touches even though he could barely move. It was a sign that he was a special player.'

On 9 November Ronaldo scored in a 3-2 win at Rayo Vallecano, yet after a 0-0 draw with Real Sociedad he was booed off the pitch. The comment after his debut, that scoring a quickfire double was a curse and not a blessing, rang true. His body needed time to adjust to the demands of regular club football at the highest level and time would also prove that the Real Sociedad of 2002/03 were a serious outfit. On 20 November, Ronaldo scored twice for Brazil in a friendly win in South Korea but a few days later he missed a goalless draw at the Camp Nou. The official line was that he was unwell, although some suggested he had bottled the occasion. Sporting director Jorge Valdano refuted the rumours, stating that he had 'the fever of a dinosaur'.

Following the *Clásico* stalemate, the European champions headed to Japan to face Olimpia – winners of the 2002 Copa Libertadores – for the Intercontinental Cup, and the right to be crowned the de facto world champions of club football. In Yokohama's International Stadium, Ronaldo gave Real Madrid the lead against the Paraguayans after just 14 minutes. A low, driven Roberto Carlos pass from the left was sent in the direction of Ronaldo who let the ball go across his body. He evaded the desperate lunge from the opposition defender before almost passing the ball into the bottom corner of the goal from 15 yards. Substitute Guti made the score 2-0 and gave Real Madrid their third Intercontinental Cup title, and second in five years. For Ronaldo it was a happy return to the Far East after his World Cup heroics.

After getting home Real Madrid won 5-1 in Mallorca, with Ronaldo opening the scoring. He then latched on to a loose pass, bamboozled a defender with a step-over then finished across the goalkeeper off the far post and into the net. In between league wins over Recreativo and Málaga, FIFA held their annual World Player of the Year gala at a convention centre in Madrid. Over 140 international coaches voted, leading to a shortlist featuring Ronaldo, Zinedine Zidane, and Oliver Kahn. The Brazilian was a resounding winner, garnering almost double the points of second-placed Kahn, who he had scored two goals past in the World Cup Final six months earlier. It was the third time Ronaldo had won the accolade, and the first since his injury problems in Milan. The lofty title stayed in Madrid having been won the previous year by Figo. This domination, including Zidane's position on the 2002 podium, perhaps justified Pérez's project.

Some suggested that awarding the title to Ronaldo in 2002 was merely sentimental given his plight between the two World Cup finals that so defined his career. He hardly set the world alight in club football in 2002 in terms of goals scored, yet by the time of the award in mid-December he was a champion at both club and international level. Moreover, he had been decisive in the final of both, scoring crucial goals and being voted man of the match. 'It had to be because of the World Cup,' opined Eduardo Álvarez. 'It was so unlikely that he would come back. He hadn't looked in shape and suddenly he was the top scorer, scoring twice in the final. That had more weight than his club form.'

After a 3-0 win at home to Sevilla upon the resumption of La Liga, Real Madrid were back at their fortress, destroying Valencia 4-1. The so-called 'winter champions' seemed unaffected by the Christmas break, picking up exactly where they had left off. On a rain-soaked mud-bath of a pitch, which turned the sparkling white shirts brown, the mesmerising Zidane assisted Ronaldo's goal, poking it through with his right foot to find Ronaldo behind the defence. Inevitably, he rounded the goalkeeper to finish. Six days later he scored the only goal of the game in a 1-0 win at Celta Vigo, gratefully poaching after Raúl's shot was spilled in soggy conditions. Ronaldo then scored against Athletic Bilbao in a 1-1 draw at the San Mamés Stadium. The famous forward saw plenty of the ball and even more of the overzealous Basque defenders but his goal came after Raúl had been foiled and Ronaldo opportunistically picked up the pieces.

On 8 February, Real Madrid thrashed Real Betis 4-1 at home. The visitors took the lead before conceding twice. Ronaldo then set Zidane up after a sumptuous one-two, and scored himself on the rebound from his own missed penalty. Eleven days later, at home to Borussia Dortmund, Ronaldo scored his first Champions League goal for Real. In the short-lived, bloated and unpopular format, *Los Blancos* finished top in the first group phase. The second group round had got off to an inauspicious start, and when Jan Koller put Dortmund ahead it looked like their defence of the European Cup was coming to an end. However, Raúl hit back before half-time and in the 56th minute Ronaldo crept in at the far post to slide in Zidane's cross for the winning goal.

Ronaldo scored in a 3-1 home win over Real Valladolid, ghosting in between the central defenders and then finishing in the top corner from the edge of the box. At the start of March Real Madrid led the table by a point but it wasn't all plain sailing for the striker. 'Ronaldo is the only player who is not integrated in the tasks of the team,' said an unusually outspoken Del Bosque. Míchel Salgado said, 'Ronaldo's not at his best and he knows it.' Ronaldo's response was to score a hat-trick in a 5-1 win over Alavés. The first goal was the pick of the bunch and saw Ronaldo produce four step-overs before shifting the ball into space and rifling past Dutruel with his left foot. He moved into second place in the battle for the Pichichi.

Real Madrid travelled to Moscow for a crucial Champions League match. Going into the final matchday of the group stage *Los Blancos* were second with Dortmund just a point behind. After 35 minutes in the Lokomotiv Stadium, a rare Ronaldo header gave Real the win, and passage to the knockout phase. Five days later Real recorded their fifth straight league victory. In a 2-0 success at home to Deportivo, Ronaldo assisted Zidane for the first before scoring the second himself, controlling a pass from the Frenchman with his right before passing the ball into the net with his left.

On 13 April, Ronaldo scored in a 4-2 defeat away to Real Sociedad, who were enjoying one of the best seasons in their history and proudly sat top of the league. For Real Madrid, it was only the third reverse in 29 La Liga games. However they had drawn far too many matches, nine in total, which opened the door for their unlikely rivals. As the Basques continued to thrive, commitment was questioned and Ronaldo was held up to a higher level of scrutiny than most. The following matchday saw the visit of Barcelona. Ronaldo, a former Camp Nou favourite, opened the scoring; Luis Enrique, who spent five years at Real Madrid, replied for the Catalans.

The second leg of the Champions League quarter-final, away to Manchester United, produced Ronaldo's greatest night in a Real Madrid shirt. The Spaniards had a 3-1 win from the first leg in the bag, a night when Ronaldo was booed off the pitch when he was replaced by Guti late on. How things can change in the space of a couple of weeks. Playing on the shoulder of Rio Ferdinand,

Ronaldo received a clever through ball from Guti before firing past Fabien Barthez from the edge of the box after 12 minutes to silence the Manchester crowd. Ruud van Nistelrooy equalised before half-time, but five minutes after the restart Ronaldo scored his second to extinguish the faint hope of Sir Alex Ferguson's men. An intricate move featuring Zidane and Roberto Carlos gave Ronaldo the relatively easy task of a tap-in from six yards, then Iván Helguera own goal made it 2-2 before Ronaldo completed his hat-trick on 59 minutes, stunning Barthez from more than 25 yards. Ronaldo's facial expression suggested that even he, the scorer of so many important and aesthetically pleasing goals, was blown away by his talents.

With the score 3-2 on the night, and 6-3 on aggregate to the Spanish giants, Ronaldo was withdrawn after 67 minutes, replaced by Argentine midfielder Santi Solari. As he made his way to the dugouts on the halfway line of Old Trafford's South Stand, now named after club icon Sir Bobby Charlton, Ronaldo received the ultimate accolade: a standing ovation from opposition supporters. Manchester United fans should have been reviling him for his part in ending their Champions League hopes, but the brilliance of the man, and the warmth with which he was regarded by most in the global football fraternity, afforded him a rare honour. Most football fans appreciate when they are in the presence of greatness and this was one such occasion. Real Madrid's supporters, in a small pocket in the corner of the stadium to his left, chanted his name as he walked off. He was accepted.

Two late goals from David Beckham, who would become the fourth *galáctico* within a matter of months, gave Manchester United a 4-3 win on the night, but it was Real Madrid heading to the final four and Ronaldo making the headlines. 'The hat-trick at Old Trafford is probably the most memorable game, the highest point of his Real Madrid career,' said Eduardo Álvarez. 'My best performance ... it was a beautiful open match ... it was truly spectacular,' said Ronaldo years later to Sports Bible. 'However, the best moment of that match was when I got replaced because all the people in the stadium gave me a standing ovation, my rivals were doing that. Everybody was standing, I really wasn't expecting that. I was very surprised by the spontaneity of the moment from a rival crowd. It was a truly magical moment for me, one of the most important in my life.'

Opposing defender Wes Brown, speaking to *The Guardian*'s Jamie Jackson in 2020, looked back on that night. 'The display Ronaldo put on got a standing ovation from everyone when he came off after his hat-trick,' began the Mancunian. 'The goal from 30 yards – you're thinking at the time "Go on then, that should be OK." You normally think, "Well if you are going to hit it, I'd rather you hit it from there." But he was just unstoppable. A young Ronaldo would have been even more dangerous, but it shows how good a player he was. Whenever he wanted to turn it on, he could, on any stage, in any stadium.' Real defender Fernando Hierro spoke eloquently about the occasion, 'We were all emotional about the ovation he got. Vicente del Bosque always had a sensitivity for that kind of thing: people's careers, attitudes, moods. The stadium started clapping him, and we were shocked, looking at each other thinking, "Wonderful – this for an opponent." We'll never forget it. It was a wonderful gesture from fans that are very special.' Henning Berg, by then back with Blackburn Rovers, was present in the stadium that night watching his former club's glamour tie. 'He was different class even though he was not as mobile,' said the Norwegian. 'His touch, his quality, everyone inside the stadium recognised the quality that he gave in this game.'

A 3-1 win away to Sevilla in the league was followed by a home fixture against Real Mallorca. Ronaldo opened the scoring after nine minutes and Real Madrid were cruising. Then, inexplicably, they collapsed in the second period, conceding five without reply. It was the first home defeat in the league for 49 matches. Catalan daily *El Mundo Deportivo* mischievously led with the headline 'Galactic Humiliation'.

Over eight defining days in May, Real Madrid faced Juventus over two legs in the semi-final of the Champions League. With 22 minutes on the clock Figo combined with Ronaldo and Morientes, the Brazilian striker putting the finishing touches on a great move, deceiving the great Gianluigi Buffon who appeared to have been expecting the ball to go across him instead of low by his left hand. David Trezeguet equalised for Juve but Roberto Carlos grabbed the winner on the night.

In Turin, Ronaldo, carrying a slight knock to his left calf following a tackle by Mark Iuliano in the first leg, started on the bench. By half-time goals from Trezeguet and Alessandro Del Piero had given the Italians a 2-0 lead, and they had their nose in front on aggregate. In the 52nd minute Del Bosque sent on Ronaldo in place of his compatriot Flávio Conceição in an attacking move. Real Madrid now needed an away goal just to force extra time. Just 13 minutes after his introduction, Ronaldo was hauled down by Uruguayan hardman Paolo Montero. Buffon, however, easily saved Figo's tame spot-kick. 'Many of us wonder why Ronaldo didn't take the penalty,' lamented Eduardo Álvarez. After 73 minutes, Pavel Nedvěd made it three for Juve, and Real now needed two and were staring down the barrel. Zidane pulled one back in the 89th minute but the Spanish side were unable to grab the decisive second, and it was Juventus who progressed to an all-Italian final against AC Milan. 'It's such a pity we didn't win the Champions League that season,' said Eduardo Álvarez. 'That was the season to win it.'

Real notched up three points on the road with a 2-1 win over Valencia, courtesy of a Ronaldo double, then recorded a stunning 4-0 win in the Madrid derby at the Vicente Calderón Stadium. Atlético had the chance to put a spanner in the works of their rivals' title challenge but they failed miserably. Ronaldo's clever movement sprung the offside trap and after controlling Zidane's slide-rule pass he smashed the ball in at the goalkeeper's near post. Raúl doubled the lead and then on the half-hour mark Ronaldo made it three, tapping in Roberto Carlos's drilled cross at the far post. Raúl completed the rout after 70 minutes.

The La Liga campaign went down to the wire and Real Madrid headed into the final day just two points ahead of surprise package Real Sociedad, who had finished the previous season in a lowly 13th place. The Basque side hosted Madrid rivals Atlético at the Anoeta Stadium, needing to win while hoping Real lost at home to Athletic Bilbao. However, Ronaldo had other ideas. Nine minutes into the final match of the season he scored from close range following great work from Roberto Carlos down the left. A goal from each side made it 2-1 to the hosts, before Ronaldo, once again sporting the iconic and lucky triangular patch of hair at the front of his head, made it 3-1 from a Zidane pass. The party was now in full swing and Real Sociedad's easy 3-0 win at home to Atlético was rendered relatively meaningless; the domestic title was returning to the Bernabéu.

Ronaldo ended the season with 23 league goals and 30 in all competitions. It was a very good return, one befitting a world-class striker. In the space of 12 months he had won the World Cup, Intercontinental Cup, and now the Spanish domestic title. There was no disputing that the FIFA World Player of the Year was back to his best. Despite this, throughout the season, whenever he was enduring a barren spell, question marks would arise about his weight. However, his record of more than 40 appearances shows that his physical condition wasn't an issue. 'He had two or three matches in which he looked unstoppable,' said Eduardo Álvarez. 'At these points, he was closer to the shape he should have had as a professional footballer and was just unstoppable.'

Despite early grumblings that he wouldn't be compatible with Raúl, the two struck up a good partnership. The knee injuries, and the imbalance Ronaldo would bring to an already stacked forward line, were doubts raised at the outset of his Real Madrid career that were put to bed. For many the fee had been too high, yet Pérez always believed that big stars eventually paid for themselves. It was a new era of sports marketing and Real Madrid's avant-garde president was at the forefront. The shirt sales alone were staggering: 2,000 in the first seven hours, 60,000 after three weeks, and 120,000 after five.

* * *

The morning after the night before. A wild party at Ronaldo's house meant that many of the players reporting to the training ground on Monday, 23 June were nursing hangovers. The trophy parade took them to the Catedral de Santa María via the city council's headquarters. On the same day, the stars learned that Del Bosque would be relieved of his duties, and stalwart Hierro's contract wouldn't be renewed. German coach Jupp Heynckes had been dismissed by former president Lorenzo Sanz in 1998 after winning the Champions League but failing to land the domestic title. For Del Bosque, the opposite was true. For the moustachioed manager, a legend of the club as a player and now successful coach, failure in Europe – despite the La Liga trophy and Intercontinental Cup – would prove to be his undoing. This shift perhaps showed that the Champions League was increasingly becoming the number one competition for clubs, in terms of prestige and finance, and Pérez refused to be left behind by Europe's elite. It was especially pertinent for Real Madrid given their historic association with the continent's flagship knockout tournament, which stretched back to 1955 when they won the inaugural version before defending it four times in a row.

Ronaldo would never have it so good again at Real Madrid. 'His most beloved coach was Del Bosque, who understood very well the player's mentality in general,' began Eduardo Álvarez. 'He knew when to intervene and when not to, and for the most part, he allowed Ronaldo freedom. Del Bosque has spoken about Ronaldo many times, discussing how his natural talent means he doesn't need coaching as much, it's more about creating the environment to allow him to flourish. He would turn a blind eye to certain things but also knew where to draw the line.'

* * *

Del Bosque's replacement was Carlos Queiroz, who had just spent a season as Sir Alex Ferguson's assistant at Old Trafford. The Portuguese was hardly the most charismatic of men but he was highly regarded, intelligent, and well-travelled as a coach. The fact he spoke several languages was a bonus given Real Madrid's assortment of stars from across the globe. One week earlier, Beckham had swapped the red of Manchester United with the all-white of Real Madrid, becoming Pérez's fourth marquee signing in as many summers. If people had questioned how much of a factor marketing was in Ronaldo's transfer, their suspicions went into overdrive with the transfer of the English megastar.

As the previous season hadn't ended until 22 June, Brazil manager Carlos Alberto Parreira omitted Ronaldo and other stars from the Confederations Cup, preferring them to rest ahead of crucial World Cup qualifiers. The break suited Ronaldo, who returned to pre-season training 5kg lighter. The unsettled Morientes left Real Madrid – joining Monaco on loan – so the Brazilian got his hands on his favoured number nine shirt. Morientes, initially offered to Inter as a makeweight in the Ronaldo deal, hadn't forgotten the previous summer in which a proposed move to Barcelona also collapsed. The animosity remained. The striker ultimately suffered from Ronaldo's arrival and was part of a sidelined middle class of players at the club who fell between the cracks; they were neither Zidanes nor Pavones.

Early silverware in 2003/04 came in the form of the Supercopa de España; Ronaldo scored in the second-leg victory over Real Mallorca. The title defence also started well with an opening-day victory at home to Real Betis. Ronaldo set Beckham up for a dream start before the visitors equalised, but Ronaldo sealed the points, bursting the net with a side-footed volley from Zidane's cross. After an away draw in Villarreal, Ronaldo linked up with his international team-mates to participate in the first match of the epic CONMEBOL World Cup qualifying series. Brazil were the first champions to have to qualify, but Ronaldo helped Parreira's men start with a bang, scoring in a 2-1 win over Colombia in sweaty Barranquilla. Back in Madrid he got the final goal in a 7-2 demolition of Real Valladolid, chopping the ball inside with his right foot before going across the goalkeeper with his left.

Three days later, Real Madrid opened their continental campaign with a 4-2 win at home to Marseille. Ronaldo made it 2-1, finishing Salgado's cross from close range. He then turned to the crowd, using his thumbs to point to the name on the back of his shirt as if to remind them who he was. After a jinking run by Zidane the ball found its way to the number nine, who finished from 20 yards to score Real's third. The goals kept on coming; Ronaldo scored in a 3-1 win in Málaga, a brace to seal victory over Espanyol, one in a 2-0 win in Vigo, two in a 3-0 home win over Athletic, and Real Madrid's only goal in a 4-1 defeat away to Sevilla.

Internationally, after four points from two qualifiers, Brazil hosted Uruguay in Curitiba; in a 3-3 draw Ronaldo scored twice. The second was a landmark 50th international goal in just 74 caps.

On matchday five of the Champions League group stage, Ronaldo scored the winner in a 2-1 victory in Marseille. Showing superb movement in the penalty area, he found some space to poke home Raúl's cut-back. Real ultimately topped the group, unbeaten in six games, to reach the round of 16. Ronaldo scored in a 1-1 draw at Osasuna and then a 2-0 win in the Madrid derby saw *Los Merengues* go top of the table. Ronaldo opened the scoring after just 15 seconds to notch his 11th league goal of the campaign. Picking the ball up 30 yards from goal, with as many as eight rival players in proximity, Ronaldo confused most of the Atlético players before powering through the backline, composing himself to finish when faced with the goalkeeper. The goal was a mixture of strength, bull-like brute force and a calm head in front of goal. In other words, classic Ronaldo.

Three days later Real travelled to the Catalan capital, Ronaldo scoring the winner in a 2-1 victory. Barcelona committed the cardinal sin of leaving him alone in the penalty box, his deflected shot giving a young Víctor Valdés little chance. It was Real Madrid's first league win at the Camp Nou in 20 years. Ronaldo scored in a 2-1 home win over Deportivo, gratefully tapping in a Zidane cross, and a day later Real were once again heavily represented at FIFA's annual awards, this time in Basel, Switzerland. Ronaldo finished third in the World Player of the Year vote, passing the baton to Zinedine Zidane. Showing the club's prowess, Roberto Carlos, David Beckham, and Raúl were also all in the top ten. Before the Christmas break there was still time for another three points, and another Ronaldo goal, in a 3-1 win away to Mallorca. Real had lost just twice in 17 league games – with only three draws – and were well placed to retain their Spanish crown.

In January Real faced Eibar in the last 16 of the Copa del Rey. After a 1-1 draw in the first leg in the tiny but charming Ipurúa Municipal Stadium, *Los Blancos* won 2-0 at home with Ronaldo and Figo getting the goals. Ronaldo scored in a 1-1 league draw at Real Betis, drawing the goalkeeper out to the edge of the box before beating him with a step-over and finishing from a tight angle. He then scored the opener in a 3-0 home win over Valencia in the Copa del Rey quarter-final first leg. The following week Real Madrid won 2-1 in the Mestalla to progress to the final four where they beat Sevilla to reach the final.

The next six league matches gleaned an impressive 16 points for Real. Ronaldo scored in five of those games, adding seven to his tally in the battle for the Pichichi. However, he missed the Copa del Rey Final on 17 March in Barcelona's Olympic Stadium, having picked up an injury, and watched from the stands. It was a close defeat – 3-2 after extra time – after which the season began to unravel. A 4-2 defeat against Athletic Bilbao scuppered their La Liga campaign, but victory over Monaco in the first leg of the Champions League quarter-final looked promising. Ronaldo made it 4-1 after 81 minutes and the home side looked to have one foot in the final four. Then loanee Morientes, facing his parent club, grabbed what at first appeared to be a slightly awkward consolation a couple of minutes later.

Before the Monaco return, Real bounced back in their fight for La Liga, winning 5-1 against Sevilla at the Bernabéu. On a rainy night in the capital Ronaldo headed in Beckham's cross for his side's second; he finished off the scoring in the dying embers of the game after dispossessing an indecisive defender before easily beating the deflated goalkeeper in a one-on-one.

On 6 April, Real travelled to the principality to face Monaco for a place in the Champions League semi-final. When Raúl scored after 36 minutes, after a Ronaldo cross and a clever dummy by Guti, his side had a healthy aggregate lead and less than an hour to protect it. Ludovic Giuly pulled one back for Monaco late in the first half and, rather embarrassingly, Morientes scored three minutes after the restart. When Giuly grabbed his second of the night on 66 minutes it put Monaco ahead on the away goal rule. The capitulation was a disaster for Real and the Morientes factor a cruel, or hilarious, irony, depending on your outlook, given he was deemed surplus to requirements by his parent club.

Out of both cups, the remaining seven league games proved disastrous for Queiroz's men, with just one win against six defeats.

Toe-poking Brazil through to the 2002 World Cup Final at the expense of Turkey.

Scoring past Oliver Kahn in the Yokohama final.

In tears, waiting for the final whistle.

Wearing no. 11 for new club, Real Madrid.

Back in Yokohama, scoring for Real Madrid in the Intercontinental Cup victory over South American champions, Olimpia.

Leaving the Old Trafford pitch to a standing ovation despite dumping the home side out of the 2002/03 Champions League.

The record-breaking goal. Ronaldo becomes the all-time leading scorer at World Cups after finding the net against Ghana.

Now a Milan player, celebrating after scoring against his old club in the derby.

At 31, and after a third major knee surgery in Paris, the European journey is over.

In full Flamengo gear, Ronaldo trains on a Rio beach as he attempts to regain full fitness. Many expected him to sign for the club he'd loved since he was a boy.

Back playing, back smiling. For Corinthians in his homeland.

With sons Alex and Ronald, at his retirement press conference.

At the Camp Nou as owner of Real Valladolid.

Promoted! Cruzeiro return to the Brazilian top flight in Ronaldo's first season as owner.

The first of the barren run was a 3-0 defeat by Osasuna at the Bernabéu. Ronaldo went off with a muscle strain after just 26 minutes, and the fans were so displeased with their evening's entertainment that the dreaded white hankies came out. Ultimately, a side that was eight points clear at one stage finished fourth in the final standings, seven points behind champions Valencia. A season that promised so much – a potential treble was still a possibility on the morning of 17 March – ended in complete, miserable failure.

Ronaldo had another stellar season on an individual note, once again appearing in more than 40 games and scoring 30 goals in all competitions. Twenty-four strikes in La Liga earned him the coveted Pichichi award for the second time in his career. Halfway through the original four-year deal signed in 2002, the Real Madrid hierarchy were impressed enough to offer a contract extension that would keep him at the club until 2008. Queiroz was less fortunate. Just ten months into his contract, the Portuguese coach paid for the disastrous end to the season with his job. He returned to Old Trafford to once again become Ferguson's assistant. 'The Queiroz season was traumatic because it went amazingly well until the Copa del Rey Final, after which the team collapsed completely,' said Eduardo Álvarez. 'The players were completely exhausted and it was an easygoing team that wasn't focused when it mattered.'

* * *

Back in the international world, Brazil faced Argentina in Belo Horizonte on 2 June. Ronaldo scored a hat-trick of penalties in a 3-1 win, the points taking Brazil above their old rival at the top of the World Cup qualification standings. Alongside Dida, Cafu,

Kaká and Roberto Carlos, Ronaldo was omitted from the Brazil squad that won the 2004 Copa América in Peru. Coach Carlos Alberto Parreira rested the quintet after an intense club season and with upcoming World Cup qualifiers in mind. 'Now, I want to enjoy my vacation, rest a bit and return in good form against Bolivia in September,' Ronaldo told the Estado news agency.

* * *

Former Real Madrid stalwart José Antonio Camacho was named as the club's new manager, for his second spell in the hotseat; his previous stint in 1998 lasted a little over three weeks after a disagreement with *Los Blancos'* hierarchy. The squad was bolstered by Argentinean central defender Walter Samuel from Roma, along with Premier League duo Michael Owen and Jonathan Woodgate from Liverpool and Newcastle United respectively.

Due to their fourth-place finish in 2003/04, Real Madrid would have to go through the qualifying stages for the Champions League and were drawn against Polish outfit Wisła Kraków in the preliminary round. Morientes, who had returned from his loan spell in Monaco, scored a brace in Poland to put his side in a strong position. Two weeks later Ronaldo grabbed a double of his own as Real won 3-1 at the Bernabéu to seal safe passage to the group stage. On the opening day of the league campaign they then won 1-0 in Mallorca. New signing Owen came off the bench to replace captain Raúl, and it was his lofted cross that found the head of Ronaldo for the winner. A 3-0 defeat to Bayer Leverkusen in the Champions League group-stage opener – and a 1-0 loss away to Espanyol – spelt the end of Camacho's short reign. The club legend, who made more than 400 appearances as a player, graciously resigned. His deputy, Mariano García

Remón, a former goalkeeper and team-mate of Camacho, took the reins.

After returning from international duty having scored in wins over Bolivia and Venezuela, Ronaldo bagged another in a 1-1 draw at Real Betis. Real's league form then picked up in the shape of four straight league wins. Ronaldo scored the second in a 2-0 home victory over Getafe, in the right place at the right time to tap-in after the goalkeeper parried Raúl's shot. He followed that up with two in a 6-1 thumping of Albacete. Ronaldo was yellow-carded in a crushing 3-0 defeat at the Camp Nou at the hands of Frank Rijkaard's resurgent and rampant Barcelona, yet he and his team bounced back immediately, steamrolling Levante 5-0. The first of his two goals saw him chest down a pass, holding off a defender with his strength before finishing with his left foot. In the final game of the Champions League's group phase, Ronaldo scored in a 3-0 win over a hapless Roma in the Stadio Olimpico. Real progressed to the last 16 from a tight group in which just a point separated the top three teams.

The final league game before the Christmas break was a 1-0 home defeat to Sevilla. The day before, a board meeting ended in an agreement that Arrigo Sacchi would be installed as the club's new director of football. The iconic Italian had finished his legendary coaching career three years earlier, following a disappointing stint at Parma. Sacchi's first piece of business saw him sideline incumbent coach Remón. Like Camacho before him, he was retained by Real, albeit in a different capacity. A press conference on Thursday, 30 December saw Vanderlei Luxemburgo installed as *Los Blancos'* third coach of the season. The 52-year-old Brazilian quit Santos, signing an 18-month contract at the Bernabéu. The only acquisition of the winter transfer window was Danish midfielder Thomas Gravesen from Everton.

The 'new manager bounce' was evident as Real Madrid won seven straight league games after Christmas. The first was a bizarre 2-1 win over Real Sociedad, the first 86 minutes of which had already taken place a few weeks earlier. Ronaldo had scored their goal, and it was 1-1 when the match was halted by the referee. Someone claiming to represent Basque separatist group ETA called in a bomb scare and the stadium was evacuated. 'We were scared to death,' defender Iván Helguera told reporters. 'It's a shame that sports and politics get mixed up.' Thankfully it proved to be a hoax and the remaining minutes were scheduled for 5 January 2005. Played at a frantic pace, as Real searched for a winner in front of thousands of fans, Ronaldo picked the ball up on the edge of the area. Squaring up the defender, his trademark step-over bamboozled his opponent. He was felled; Zidane stepped up to finish the penalty and claim the three points. Ronaldo then scored twice in a 3-0 win away to Atlético, the first coming in the 14th minute after a cheeky dummy by Zidane. Atlético laid siege to Real Madrid's goal, and it wasn't until late that the visitors were able to seal the victory through Solari and Ronaldo's second. He then scored in a 3-1 win at home to Real Zaragoza.

Under his compatriot Luxemburgo, Ronaldo seemed to be highly motivated, working with a fitness coach and a nutritionist to shed 6kg. However, controversy wasn't far away. Ronaldo was conspicuous by his absence in a 2-0 home defeat to Athletic Bilbao on 19 February after he returned to Madrid late from a short break in France. Five days earlier, on Valentine's Day, Ronaldo and his fiancée – Brazilian model and TV host Daniella Cicarelli – hosted an extravagant bash at a chateau in Chantilly. The ceremony was initially intended to be a wedding, but it was downgraded to an engagement celebration after it transpired Ronaldo's divorce from Milene Domingues hadn't been finalised before a certain deadline to allow him to freely re-marry. They also hadn't given the local council sufficient notice to obtain a marriage certificate in any case. The party reportedly cost €700,000. Just three months later, the engagement was off.

Ronaldo scored his first goal for almost two months in a 1-1 draw with Real Betis. Four days later, Real Madrid faced Juventus in the second leg of the Champions League last 16. Leading 1-0 from the first leg, and with the score goalless, Ronaldo – who was all smiles before kick-off – tested Gianluigi Buffon six minutes into the second half, his shot being tipped on to the post after a powerful run from the halfway line. Juventus scored, meaning it was 1-1 on aggregate, and the game went to extra time. As a Real Madrid attack was being mounted, Ronaldo lashed out at Alessio Tacchinardi. Austrian referee Markus Merk took advice from his assistant before rightly showing Ronaldo the red card, just the second of his career. The Old Lady grabbed a winner in extra time.

Luxemburgo's men, suffering from a hangover after their European exit, then lost 2-1 at Getafe. However they finished the season in impressive fashion, dropping just four points in the final ten games. Ronaldo was on fire during the stunning run, scoring nine times. Revenge was gained over Barcelona in Madrid with Ronaldo scoring the second in a 4-2 win. He added a double in a 2-0 win at Levante, one in a 2-1 home win over Villarreal, a brace at Real Sociedad in another 2-0 win on the road, and two in a 5-0 mauling of Racing Santander at the Bernabéu. It was the fifth straight game in which he'd scored. On the final day of the season, a 3-1 win away to Real Zaragoza, Ronaldo found the target again.

Real finished the season comfortably in second place, four points off Barcelona. The form since Luxemburgo arrived represented a massive improvement, from 1.81 points per game in the first portion of the season to 2.32 after his appointment. If that form had been extrapolated over the 38-game schedule it would have been enough to win the league. Ronaldo's haul of 21 goals in La Liga was four short of Diego Forlán's Pichichi-winning 25, but another impressive season nonetheless. It was the third campaign in which he'd clocked more than 40 appearances.

* * *

The squad was renovated in the summer of 2005. Santi Solari, Luís Figo and Walter Samuel joined Inter while Michael Owen headed for Newcastle United. Real Madrid's highest-profile signings included young defender Sergio Ramos from Sevilla, and Brazilian duo Robinho and Júlio Baptista.

On the opening day of the 2005/06 season Ronaldo scored in a 2-1 win away to Cádiz. Receiving a pass with his back to goal more than 25 yards out, he allowed a defender to get tight before spinning him and almost side-footing the ball into the bottom corner from outside the box. In the following game he netted from the spot in a 3-2 home reverse to Celta Vigo, and on matchday five Ronaldo scored a double in a 3-0 win away to Alavés. The first was a thumping half volley from just outside the D. He then opened the scoring in a 4-0 win over rock-bottom Mallorca in the capital with another superb strike from outside the box.

Upon his return from international duty, having scored in a win for Brazil who completed their qualifying campaign top of the group to reach the World Cup, Ronaldo scored twice in a 3-0 win in the Madrid derby. The first came from the penalty spot; the second, on the hour, was passed into the corner beyond the goalkeeper to make it 2-0.

On 19 November, champions Barcelona travelled to Madrid. It was a routine 3-0 victory for the purring Catalan outfit, so much so that Ronaldinho, scoring what proved to be the final goal in the 77th minute, was applauded by the Bernabéu crowd. It was a great sporting gesture yet also an admonishment to Real's players. The jeering of the men in white showed that, to the fans in the stands, it wasn't acceptable for their team to roll over for anyone, especially not Barcelona.

Two days after Real Madrid had beaten Getafe 1-0 at home, Vanderlei Luxemburgo was sacked. According to the Brazilian coach, Florentino Pérez criticised his decision to remove scorer Ronaldo in the 90th minute – claiming it wasn't in the club's spirit to hold out for a result against the likes of Getafe, even though Madrid were down to ten men following David Beckham's dismissal. Arrigo Sacchi, who ultimately proved to be a failed experiment, left at the same time. Juan Ramón López Caro was promoted from within to lead the team until the end of the season.

Four days before Christmas, Ronaldo scored in a 2-1 defeat at home to Racing Santander. His next goal came on 4 February, in a 4-0 win over Espanyol, as he headed in from Cicinho's cross. Ten days later Ronaldo scored in a 4-0 win over Real Zaragoza, although Real Madrid exited the Copa del Rey after the humiliating 6-1 defeat in the first leg at La Romareda, their heaviest loss for seven years.

In late February 2006, major news rocked Madrid: Florentino Pérez had resigned. The outgoing president cited defeat to Mallorca the night before as the final straw, proof that his philosophy was no longer working. The Pérez era began in 2000 when he unseated the incumbent Lorenzo Sanz, and in 2004 he was re-elected with a whopping 94.2 per cent of the votes. There were early triumphs on the pitch, and there's no doubt it was off the pitch where he made profound and successful changes in the club's structure. However, the years before his departure saw a revolving door of managers fail to halt a relentless Barcelona, who were ten points in front at the time of his resignation. Real were almost three years without a trophy, and 1-0 down to Arsenal after the first leg of their Champions League last-16 tie. 'I believe we need a change of direction,' the 58-year-old said. 'Having analysed the situation I considered that this was the time for me to step down. I believe this will be a change for the best. It is a decision I have thought hard about.' Fernando Martín, the vice-president, was the unanimous choice of the board to take over from Pérez.

On 8 March, a goalless draw in London confirmed Real's exit from European competition after what for Ronaldo was a dismal Champions League campaign in which he made just two appearances and failed to score. Fourteen days later he did add an injury-time equaliser in a 1-1 draw in Zaragoza; he also opened the scoring in a 4-0 home win over Deportivo. On the first day in April, Real Madrid travelled to the Camp Nou. The visitors looked to be heading for another embarrassing *Clásico* defeat when Roberto Carlos was red-carded and Ronaldinho netted the subsequent penalty. However, Ronaldo equalised after latching on to Baptista's pass and, waiting for Víctor Valdés to blink first, delicately chipped the goalkeeper. Real were 11 points off the pace with seven fixtures remaining so the rest of the campaign was more about salvaging pride than anything else.

Ronaldo scored in a 1-1 draw at home to Real Sociedad before limping off with an injury to his right thigh that curtailed his season. *Los Blancos* ended the campaign in second place, 12 points off Frank Rijkaard's champions. Although they only suffered one defeat after Pérez left, they also drew seven.

For Ronaldo, it was the first season in four years at Real Madrid in which he'd failed to make more than 40 appearances; this time it was less than 30. 'It wasn't good by his standards,' said Eduardo Álvarez. 'He'd picked up several injuries; his body was falling apart. He also hadn't taken care of himself for a while. And then, in comes [Fabio] Capello.' The Italian, known for his strict disciplinary code, would, perhaps predictably, not see eye to eye with Ronaldo. However, with the summer of 2006 approaching, there was just one thought on the forward's mind: representing his country at what would surely be his last World Cup. In a dream world, he'd not only win the trophy for a third time, but overtake Just Fontaine and Gerd Müller to become the highest scorer in the history of the competition.

Chapter 10

The End of the Affair

BRAZIL QUALIFIED for the 2006 World Cup in Germany with relative ease, finishing joint top of the CONMEBOL table – alongside Argentina – with 34 points. The two couldn't be separated by the head-to-head results, and both conceded 17 in 18 games. Brazil, however, scored six more than the *Albiceleste* and therefore edged out their rivals on goals scored. Brazil lost just twice during qualifying, and the five-time winners kept up their impressive record of being the only team to have qualified for every World Cup. Ronaldo was the top scorer during the campaign with ten goals, three more than his nearest rival, Argentina's Hernán Crespo.

The team was led by legendary figure Carlos Alberto Parreira, who had led Brazil to glory in the 1994 World Cup. Parreira was on Brazil's coaching staff in Mexico in 1970 and managed three Middle Eastern nations – Kuwait (1982), UAE (1990) and Saudi Arabia (1998) – at FIFA's flagship global tournament. He was back in charge of Brazil for the third time and since returning in 2003 he had led the side to the Copa América in 2004 as well as the Confederations Cup the following year.

Brazil were the highest-ranked team at the tournament in Germany, and odds-on favourites with many bookmakers.

Although there were also ten players in the squad aged 30 or over, the 29-year-old Ronaldo was one of the elder statesmen in terms of international experience. Only Cafu – the sole man to have appeared in three consecutive World Cup finals – and Roberto Carlos had more caps than the forward, who was participating in his fourth World Cup.

With the magic quartet of Ronaldo, Adriano, Kaká and Ronaldinho, there was much pre-tournament hype. 'The current generation is spectacular, perhaps the best,' said Flávio Orro of TV Globo, hyperbolically. 'If Ronaldo hasn't worn himself out during the season, he can really put on a show. He can become the top scorer in World Cups and equal Pelé by winning his third. I'm backing him and Brazil to pull it off.'

At the end of May, Ronaldo already knew he would be in the starting XI for the opening match, despite not having played for Real Madrid since 8 April when he limped out of their 1-1 draw with Real Sociedad with a thigh strain. Not for the first time in his career there were question marks over his fitness and weight. 'When he won the World Cup, he was getting rid of this huge albatross around his neck and he just kind of like relaxed,' said Fernando Duarte, who began his journalism career with Rio newspaper *O Globo* in 1996. 'Ronaldo was not as motivated as he was in 2002. He was overweight, partying way too much, and not in the best shape. His weight became this huge subject. Before the World Cup, he was even being taunted by the Real Madrid fans who were calling him *gordo*.'

A frustrated Ronaldo hit out at reporters, 'It doesn't bother me in the slightest. I think it's all down to a lack of knowledge. After all, what is fat. People have been talking about it for so long that nowadays I just take it as a joke. Nobody ever talks about exact numbers, about the percentage of fat. It's down to a lack of knowledge, a lack of information and a lack of something better to talk about.' However, Ronaldo, who had trained in full since reporting for international duty, appeared in a positive frame of mind, 'This is like a pre-season for me, I'm coming back from injury and I haven't played for one and a half months. I'm very happy and I'm getting on with my job.'

Having previously been more than happy to make predictions about goals at past tournaments, now he was more experienced he was a little more reserved. 'It's very difficult to make a forecast,' he began. 'The principal target is the collective triumph, to help Brazil win a sixth World Cup. My personal success takes a back seat. In any case, if I score goals, I'll be helping Brazil to win the title.' In the past Ronaldo had never been shy in making predictions, but he had mellowed in this regard. 'But announcing the goals, the awards?' he wrote in a 2015 article for the Players' Tribune. 'I was just doing what I had seen other guys doing when I was growing up. The bragging … the showmanship … it took me a couple of years – probably longer than it should have – to realise, this isn't me. It wasn't my personality to be the type of player who spoke like that. At the end of the day, I could just let my game do the talking.'

Brazil played their final warm-up match against New Zealand in Geneva. Ronaldo opened the scoring in a 4-0 win before being replaced by Robinho at half-time. Before the game against the All Whites he had complained about blisters and pain in his feet, to the extent that Real Madrid sent him some worn-in boots.

Three days before Brazil were due to open their campaign in Berlin's Olympiastadion, there were still question marks over his condition. 'I've come here, I've been training and working, it's normal I might have been a little above my normal weight when I arrived but that's gone down with the training,' said a prickly Ronaldo. 'However, the media insist it's still a problem and the blisters are still a problem. What difference does it make if I'm one kilo overweight? They [the media] have been talking about this nonsense for three years. This doesn't interest anyone; it isn't of public interest. It's daft.'

On 13 June, Brazil kicked off against Croatia. Just before half-time their young superstar Kaká, who would be the undisputed best player in the world in 2007, scored the only goal of the game with a sublime left-footed finish. Ronaldo – not operating at 100 per cent – was replaced by Robinho after 69 minutes. Five days later, at the Allianz Arena, Brazil clocked up another win and another clean sheet. Adriano scored the first against Australia, a goal assisted by Ronaldo, who was substituted for Gilberto Silva after 72 minutes. Lyon striker Fred rounded off the scoring late in the game.

The *Seleção* faced Japan in Dortmund in their final group-stage game. The Asian side took the lead, but Ronaldo equalised on the stroke of half-time. Ronaldinho picked out Cicinho who nodded across the box for Ronaldo to head home. His 13th World Cup goal took him past Pelé in the all-time list, and level with France's Just Fontaine. He also joined an exclusive club, becoming the 20th player to score in three World Cups. Despite his problems, and his peak being a distant speck in the rear-view mirror, he was still one of the world's best strikers. Lyon's Juninho Pernambucano and Gilberto of Hertha Berlin gave Brazil a 3-1 lead before Ronaldo got his second. Exchanging passes with Juan, who had burst out of defence with the ball, he finished from the edge of the D, past the outstretched left hand of Japan's goalkeeper. He now had 14

World Cup goals, joint first with Germany's Gerd Müller in the all-time list.

Brazil topped the group with maximum points, scoring seven and conceding just one. Against Japan, Ronaldo completed his first full 90 minutes of the tournament. On the surface it boded well for the knockout stage, where in the last 16 Ghana would be their opponents in Dortmund. After just five minutes, Ronaldo opened the scoring. Kaká's pass found the striker – who had beaten the offside trap – in space with just the goalkeeper to beat. A step-over left the Ghanaian number one on his backside, allowing Ronaldo to finish into the empty net. With 15 goals, it made him the outright highest scorer in World Cup history. Adriano and Ze Roberto also scored to make it 3-0 and maintain their perfect record against African teams in World Cups. Despite criticism back home, Parreira's team had won four out of four and appeared to be clicking.

However, it all came unstuck in a lacklustre team performance against France in the quarter-final in Frankfurt. Zinedine Zidane was stupendous for *Les Bleus*, giving Brazil a painful reminder of the final in Paris eight years earlier. It was Zidane's free kick which set up Thierry Henry to volley the winner past Dida, and Fabien Barthez denied Ronaldo late on to keep a clean sheet and ensure victory for the French. Ronaldo was booked on a frustrating evening. 'That game against France was more painful than the 7-1 [versus Germany in the 2014 home World Cup semi-final],' said Fernando Duarte, who has covered Brazil at four World Cups and two Olympics. 'We never threatened them. It looked like Zidane was doing whatever he wanted. He showboated and at one point even flicked the ball over Ronaldo's head.'

Ronaldo was awarded the bronze shoe, having scored three goals and assisted one in 409 minutes of football. Yet Brazil's defence of their trophy was over. Ronaldo's 97th cap would be his last competitive appearance for Brazil; the strike against Ghana was his 62nd international goal, the last time he would hit the back of the net in the famous yellow shirt.

Brazil had flattered to deceive when it mattered. 'The side were top-heavy and unconvincing,' wrote Tim Vickery in his ESPN column. 'No one came out of it well.' Ten days after Italy lifted the World Cup having beaten France on penalties in the final, Parreira resigned. A statement from the CBF read, 'The coach says he needs to dedicate time to his family after four years leading the Brazilian national team. It was a joint decision and Parreira will no longer have any connection with the Brazilian Football Confederation.'

Duarte, the author of the 2014 book *Shocking Brazil: Six Games that Shook the World Cup*, believes there were numerous problems, 'They won the Confederations Cup [in June 2005], thrashing Argentina in the final. The funny thing is in that tournament Ronaldo wasn't there, Cafu wasn't there; some of the big stars had been rested. So, there was a huge debate in Brazil as to why aren't we giving these new guys a chance to get more space in this team. Asking why the team wasn't being built around Adriano, instead of Ronaldo, and why Cafu and Roberto Carlos were still playing.

'There was a feeling that the class of 2002 had gone soft, that they were in exhibition mode. They weren't motivated like they were in 2002 when there was the ghost of 1998. They were hungry, they had lost the final in a bad way, and they were drubbed. At the time it was Brazil's worst defeat in a World Cup. It's like the hunger wasn't there in 2006. There was a transition that needed to be done between 2002 and 2006 between the old guys and the new guys and I don't think Parreira handled that quite well enough. There was a party atmosphere that permeated the team – even the guys that hadn't won stuff. It wasn't just him. The whole team had problems. But it didn't help that our supposed main goal threat was not at the peak of his powers. But neither was Adriano. Ronaldinho was burnt out, he was jaded. He was another problem. The team was badly prepared and some of the main stars including Ronaldo were far from their peak physical prowess. He was nowhere near the condition that would give him a chance to be his best at that tournament.'

As popular as Ronaldo was, and remains, he, like other football heroes, is not beyond criticism in a country where football is akin to a religion. 'It kind of like was an end of the affair between Ronaldo and the Brazilian public,' said Duarte. 'He's still an idol but Brazilians were kind of like, "Thank you for your service but enough is enough." His credibility was badly damaged by that World Cup. People look at him as a legend. These guys will always command some kind of fandom but they're not untouchable figures.'

However, Duarte – who at the time of publication lived in the south of England and worked for the BBC World Service – still speaks fondly of the man who, until surpassed by Neymar, was second only to Pelé in Brazil's all-time scoring list, 'He's always going to have 2002. The redemption, the exorcism of his demons. He didn't kick a ball for two years, then boom, wins the World Cup, top scorer, first to score more than six goals in ages. He missed the chance to go out with a bang in 2006. But how can I criticise a guy who survived so many things? But he let himself down in that World Cup. It looked like he was there just for who he was, he didn't look after himself. It's a shame he didn't make that final effort. But I thank him for the memories. In my life, of the players I've seen, he's surely one of the best.'

For Ronaldo, it was time to return to Madrid. After a frustrating club campaign last time out, and a World Cup to forget – aside from the individual record – the Bernabéu would be no haven. Winds of change were blowing a howling, frosty, gale through the famous old club, and the popular forward would soon be left in the cold.

Chapter 11

San Siro Return

RONALDO RETURNED from the 2006 World Cup complaining of pain in his knees and was subsequently missing from club action until November. Real Madrid – now under Fabio Capello, the seventh coach Ronaldo had worked with since joining in 2002 – were flying, having lost just one of the first eight league games, a run which, crucially, included a home win over Barcelona.

His first goal of the season came at the Bernabéu on 9 November in the second leg of the Copa del Rey round of 32 as Real eased to a 5-1 win over modest Écija. It was a measured finish with his left foot, steered into the bottom corner from the edge of the box. His first league goal of the campaign came at home to Athletic Bilbao on 3 December. With his team 1-0 down he equalised with a trademark goal. A raking pass from near the halfway line was sent over the top and he evaded the two central defenders, taking a touch and then sliding it through the goalkeeper's legs. It was a mesmerising individual performance; Ronaldo looked like he thoroughly enjoyed himself. Roberto Carlos later grabbed the winner.

Ronaldo scored twice as Real drew 2-2 with Dynamo in Kyiv. It was the final game of the Champions League group stage and

Los Blancos qualified in second place despite being 2-0 down. Ronaldo was thwarted in the 85th minute and three defenders were required to stop him from taking a shot on goal. However, from the resulting corner he turned the ball in from close range. Barely a minute later Ronaldo, with more keen marking from the Ukrainians, was taken down in the box. He coolly converted the penalty, sending the goalkeeper the wrong way.

Back in La Liga, against Deportivo La Coruña on 7 January 2007, Ronaldo came off the bench to replace Guti in the 57th minute although the damage had been done and his side fell 2-0. It was Real's fourth league defeat in nine games and Ronaldo's last appearance for the club; AC Milan, and a San Siro return, beckoned.

Despite something of a resurgence towards the end of the year, Ronaldo's relationship with Capello was frosty and was never destined to work given their opposing personality types. The forward aimed a swipe at his boss as he was on his way to the airport, bound for Milan, 'I would like to thank the fans who've supported me all the time and thank all the team-mates that I've had here and all the coaches I've had – except one. It's sad because I've been here four and a half years, but now I've got another important challenge in my life and that is to succeed in Milan. It breaks your heart, but that's life. It is a shame. I never had any problems with the coach, but he didn't want me and as I'm a professional I wanted to carry on playing and so we looked for another solution.' Capello, talking to Italian TV channel Telelombardia, hit back immediately, 'I wish him the best of luck in doing what he used to do which is being a great player.' The inference was obvious; in his mind, Ronaldo was no longer a top-drawer talent.

Ronaldo's lifestyle and weight issues were a major gripe for the Italian disciplinarian. 'He weighed 96kg, boxing stuff,' Capello told Sky Sports Italia in 2018. 'I asked him how much he weighed when he won the World Cup [in 2002] and he said 84kg, so I asked him to at least get to 88kg. It was a shame; he didn't want to make the smallest sacrifice and the best he managed was 94kg.' Capello also said Ruud van Nistelrooy, signed by Real in the summer of 2006 ostensibly to replace Ronaldo, told him that the dressing room often smelled of alcohol, suggesting that the Brazilian was the source of the stench. The Dutchman flatly denied this on Twitter in May 2020.

Ronaldo told Fox Sports in 2017 that he only left Real Madrid because of Capello, 'I didn't want to leave. I started to have a lot of problems with Capello. If I was 100g overweight, he would take me out of the team. I am tolerant, I want to understand other points of view. But with him, I just couldn't. I understand his position as the manager, but sometimes in football, 100 or 200 grams don't make the difference. It's about what you actually do, and he didn't see what I actually did, what I could contribute, as the be all and end all.'

The club's official website was gushing with praise for a player who scored 104 goals in 177 games, finishing as the leading scorer in each of his four completed seasons, 'Real Madrid would like to recognise everything that this special player has given the club during his time here. Madrid fans will never forget the moments of great football he has provided … His magic with the ball will always be remembered by Madrid's fans … an endless list of goals and memorable performances.' Ronaldo was the fifth foreigner to score over a century of goals for the club, and *Marca* named him in its Real Madrid best foreign XI.

Despite their differences, Capello, speaking in 2017 at the Football Leader conference, perhaps having mellowed with time, spoke highly of his former player, 'The most difficult to handle was the best I coached: Ronaldo, *Il Fenomeno*. He was the player who created the most problems for me in the dressing room. He used to throw parties and do everything … but if we're talking about talent then he was the greatest, without a doubt.' Journalist and Real Madrid fan Eduardo Álvarez believes Ronaldo's exit was almost inevitable given the arrival of Capello, 'The previous season hadn't been good by his standards because he'd picked up several injuries. His body was falling apart. He'd had some serious injuries and hadn't taken care of himself for a while. And then, in comes Capello.'

Álvarez suggested that Ronaldo had a huge impact on and off the pitch, and on the fans, while alluding to the fact that he might have been difficult for certain coaches, 'He was extremely gifted technically but there was an aura to him that was unrivalled and that made him incredibly successful even when he wasn't in the optimal conditions. It's impossible to be mad at him unless you're the coach. Team-mates [loved him] in a matter of days … he's so much fun, and so talented. Usually, incredibly talented players are not a lot of fun to be around. He's inventive, jokes all the time, and likes to have fun. If you're the coach, it's probably not something you enjoy. Everyone around thought it was a lot of fun apart from the coach. He has this ability to be liked by everyone. You would not hear someone speak badly about Ronaldo. Except for the coach who knew the lifestyle was not that of a top professional footballer and they were concerned that younger players were learning bad habits. Even if he missed a couple of chances, fans would never get mad at him. Very few players have this ability.

You could see they were having fun and that is so rare to see at the highest level.'

Ronaldo even directly impacted Real Madrid's style of football. 'He was so influential,' Álvarez began. 'Raúl even said that Ronaldo was so good that the team forgot how to play unless it was to find him in space. The team's efforts were directed towards finding him in space. They wouldn't use high crosses because he wasn't great in the air. Always trying to find him behind the defence. That's a huge compliment and shows how he influenced how the team played. There was no other way to play when Ronaldo was on the pitch, and this was a team containing Raúl, Figo, and Zidane, extremely talented attackers. That, to me, is amazing.

'Among Real Madrid fans, he is adored. The Bernabéu crowd can be fickle. If there are rumours that you're not taking care of yourself, they can kill you. They won't respect you. However, Ronaldo had this ability to get on the right side of people and fans would, because he was so skilled, forgive anything he did. This is extremely rare at the Bernabéu. I can't think of another player like this. They loved the way he finished. It was uncanny how he could always put the ball low, in the corner. It's unbelievable how accurate his finishing was. Pure finesse. When you're at top speed you rarely have the mindset of being cold and calculating and finish exactly where you want to put the ball. But he had cold blood. He never gets nervous or overwhelmed. He knows what he must do and just executes. It's marvellous to watch. If he came to the Bernabéu today, he would spend two hours signing autographs and that to me shows how loved he is. Lots of other former players might generate mixed feelings but Ronaldo is universally loved, missed, and cherished.'

However, like Ronaldo, Álvarez has regrets while remaining philosophical, 'The greatest shame was that he didn't win the Champions League with Real Madrid because that is always a huge thing. They were close [in 2002/03]. We had four full seasons out of him, and that's much more than people expected when he first arrived. It's a pity that he didn't follow better routines in terms of health, but I also don't think he'd be the same player if he did. He wouldn't have been as much fun, or as inventive. It goes with the package.'

On 18 January 2007, 11 days after his final appearance for *Los Blancos*, it was reported that Ronaldo had agreed terms with AC Milan, with a reported transfer fee of €7.5m plus a €500,000 add-on should his new club qualify for the Champions League at any point during his 18-month contract. 'It is a very satisfactory agreement for a top-class player,' said Milan's vice-chairman and CEO, Adriano Galliani, who reportedly fended off interest from Juventus and Saudi Arabian club Al-Ittihad to capture the signature.

Ronaldo trained with Real Madrid as usual on the morning of Thursday, 25 January, before flying to Milan. He was in the stands for the *Rossoneri*'s Coppa Italia semi-final against Roma before undergoing a medical at the Milanello training complex the next morning. The transfer was completed on Tuesday, 30 January and Ronaldo was officially a Milan player, becoming the tenth foreigner to play for both Inter and AC, joining a stellar list which included the likes of Clarence Seedorf, Hernán Crespo and Edgar Davids.

Milan needed a spark up front. Andriy Shevchenko had joined Chelsea in the summer of 2006, and between his departure and the winter break the side had scored just 22 goals in 18 league games. Incumbent forwards Filippo Inzaghi, Ricardo Oliveira and Alberto Gilardino were underperforming, and Marco Borriello was out of action having failed a drugs test in November, a ban which kept him out of action until March. 'Players who help us are always welcome,' said Inzaghi. 'We hope he [Ronaldo] will give us a big helping hand.' Kaká was also pleased to partner with his international team-mate at club level, albeit with a caveat, 'I don't need to tell anybody how important he has been to football over the last decade. I believe he still has a lot to offer if he keeps himself motivated.'

His new coach, Carlo Ancelotti, renowned for his man-management skills, knew Ronaldo was unfit but said he 'remains a great player'. He also suggested that the frontman had lost his enthusiasm at Real Madrid having been frozen out by Capello. 'Ronaldo is not fat, he is just sturdy and has an imposing figure,' Ancelotti said. 'I think his main problem was a lack of motivation but his decision to come here is a very positive sign. He hasn't trained much after being dropped by Madrid but remains an excellent player.'

In an ideal world, Ronaldo may have returned to the *Nerazzurri*. 'I did everything I could to get back to Inter,' he said following his retirement 2011. 'I waited as long as I could to give them time to say yes or no. When neither a yes nor a no comes, it means no.' Roberto Mancini's Inter, taking advantage of the sanctions suffered by their rivals following the *Calciopoli* scandal, were walking the league and on the way to winning their first title in 18 years. They boasted a formidable forward line and saw little need in adding the past-his-best Ronaldo to their ranks.

Ronaldo, although he initially favoured an Inter return, saw no problem with joining Milan once it became clear his former employers weren't interested, and he sought to win their fans over. 'There was some initial scepticism around Ronaldo from Milan fans,' began Emmet Gates, who covers Italian football for *Forbes*. 'Partly due to his past with Inter, and partly because he was out of favour at Madrid under Fabio Capello. Ronaldo was 30, and his history with knee issues meant he had a lot of mileage at that stage of his career. But most *Milanisti* recognised that if he could get something close to resembling his best, he would score goals in a team that was struggling for them in the aftermath of Andriy Shevchenko's move to Chelsea the prior summer.'

Wearing the number 99 on the back of his red and black shirt, Ronaldo made his Milan debut on 11 February 2007 as a substitute against Livorno at the San Siro. He had been unable to relieve Inzaghi of his number nine shirt, his stock having fallen considerably since he took Zamorano's over a decade earlier. Despite his previous association with Inter, Milan fans gave him a rousing ovation as he entered the pitch, replacing countryman Ricardo Oliveira with the game tied at 1-1. Eight minutes later, Marek Jankulovski grabbed the winner for AC. Speaking to Sky Italia after the game, Ancelotti was full of praise for the new man, 'He played for half an hour, created three chances, looked dangerous from long range and did very well to free himself from his markers. He must improve his physical condition, but I believe he will be very important to us. He is an incredible talent. At the moment he only shows it in flashes, but basically, he's the same player he always was – very fast, powerful, quick to react, and has wonderful technique.' During his cameo, Ronaldo forced Livorno goalkeeper Marco Amelia into a good save as he tipped the ball round the post. 'It went really well,' he said. 'I've still got a lot to learn from this group of players, but I'm pleased with the start I've made. Sooner or later the goals will come.'

And he was true to his word. In the very next game, the following Saturday at Siena, Ronaldo bagged a brace – and created a goal – in a thrilling 4-3 win. Alongside Oliveira, with Kaká – who went on to win the Ballon d'Or later in 2007 – just behind, Ronaldo formed part of an all-Brazilian forward trio. After 16 minutes he opened his Milan account, heading a clipped pass from Andrea Pirlo back across the goalkeeper. The smile returned. The home side equalised but on 29 minutes Ronaldo slid the ball into the path of Oliveira who restored the *Rossoneri's* lead. Siena pegged Milan back once again and the game remained level until the 81st minute when Ronaldo tapped in a pull-back from Kaká. Siena thought they'd earned a dramatic draw with a late equaliser but, one minute later Massimo Ambrosini's goal handed the points to the visitors. Ronaldo hinted there was more to come, 'I'm not yet in perfect physical condition. Slowly but surely, I will reach my top condition.'

Ancelotti, whose approach was in stark contrast to Capello, allowed Ronaldo to flourish. 'Two goals, an assist, 90 minutes' excellent work,' his new boss said following the Siena victory. 'Ancelotti famously tells the story of the team going to face Siena, and Ancelotti was giving a team talk and Ronaldo wasn't interested in the slightest,' recounted Emmet Gates, who has also written for *The Guardian*. 'Ancelotti asked Ronaldo about whether he wanted to know the names of the players he was facing that afternoon. Ronaldo, with that famous smile, reportedly said something along the lines of, 'No boss, but they sure know who I am.' And he scored twice because of course he did. Ancelotti at that stage knew how to handle big names, and if Ronaldo scored, he couldn't argue.'

Milan had started the season with an eight-point deduction due to their role in the *Calciopoli* match-fixing scandal, and four defeats in five during October and November, a run during which they won just one game in nine, left them dangerously close to the bottom of the table. However, the Ronaldo-inspired Siena victory was their 12th match unbeaten. Astonishingly they now occupied fifth position, just one step away from their pre-season target of fourth.

The next three matches gleaned seven points, with the defence breached just once. Ronaldo started two and was a used substitute in the other. Then, on 11 March, came the one everyone had been waiting for since the moment he returned to the San Siro: the Milan derby. To make it more hostile, Milan faced Inter as the 'away' side. Against the formidable league leaders, who lost just once all season, Ancelotti was more conservative with his line-up, selecting Kaká just off Ronaldo in a 4-4-1-1 formation. Although Mancini had expected Ancelotti to start with the Brazilian attacking trident, the Inter boss told the club's in-house station he planned for both eventualities so was fully prepared. After having a goal rightly ruled out for offside, Ronaldo then opened the scoring with a stunning strike in the 40th minute. Picking up the ball on the right-hand side following a pass from Rino Gattuso, Ronaldo drove infield before unleashing an unstoppable left-footed shot into the far corner past compatriot Júlio César from 25 yards.

Before the crunch match, Ronaldo asked the Inter fans for respect. After all, he'd spent five years in their colours and had been to hell and back during his time with them. But for those on the Curva Nord – where Inter's most hardcore and high-maintenance fans congregate – the betrayal was too much. His pleas were ignored, every touch greeted by deafening boos and jeers. According to James Richardson, writing in *The Guardian*, 30,000 plastic whistles had been distributed by the Inter ultras for maximum effect. Given the perceived lack of respect, Ronaldo enjoyed the goal, cupping his ears to taunt the Inter fans before being mobbed by his team-mates. 'It's a weird thing, we've seen the likes of Clarence Seedorf and Christian Vieri go directly between Inter and Milan, and mostly recently Hakan Çalhanoğlu, without too much of an uproar,' said Gates. 'The city neighbours are rivals, but it's not like transferring between Juventus and Napoli.'

Ronaldo's goal may have dented the pride of the *Interisti*, and bloodied Inter's nose, but they hit back in the second half through Julio Cruz and Zlatan Ibrahimović to win the match. Although they had 56 per cent possession of the ball Milan lost out to their ruthless and clinical rivals, who retained their unassailable 16-point lead over Roma at the top of the table. 'That was one of the great Milan derbies of the last 20 years, a star-studded game,' said Gates.

Milan bounced back from the derby defeat with a home win over Atalanta, before drawing 1-1 in the capital with second-placed Roma. On 7 April, Ronaldo opened the scoring in a 3-1 home win over Empoli. A Kaká pass was collected in the final third and trademark step-overs bamboozled the opposition defenders before he smashed the ball beyond the goalkeeper from ten yards. It was a goal a peak Ronaldo of a decade earlier would have been proud of.

Next, Ancelotti's men travelled to Sicily to face Messina. With his team 2-0 up through Kaká and Guiseppe Favalli, Ronaldo made it three in the 86th minute with another thunderbolt. Kaká fed the ball to Ronaldo, making a run off the forward. Ronaldo feinted as if he would return the pass but instead spun the other way, creating space for himself before lashing the ball in the top corner from the best part of 30 yards. Messina pulled a goal back but it was another win for Milan who, aside from the derby defeat the previous month, were unbeaten in the league since 11 November.

A 5-2 win over Ascoli on the road was followed by a 3-1 win over Cagliari at the San Siro. The visitors were without a win in the previous five; Milan were on a hot streak. After 13 minutes Ronaldo opened the scoring, easily turning in a low, drilled cross from Cafu. The second goal came ten minutes later, from the same source. This time Cafu's cross was a deeper one, sailing over the flapping goalkeeper and on to Ronaldo's head. A 1-0 win away at Torino was Milan's sixth in seven games and Ronaldo started each of these, operating in a 4-3-1-2 formation alongside Oliveira or Gilardino, with Kaká behind pulling the strings. Four goals in that spell showed that Ronaldo – visibly enjoying the confidence being shown in him by Ancelotti – could still operate at the top level when fit.

The wheels fell off slightly, however, as Milan failed to win any of the last four league games. Coincidentally Ronaldo missed three of them. However the *Rossoneri*, despite starting the season with a points handicap, had qualified for the Champions League with three points to spare. Ancelotti had kept his promise and Ronaldo's arrival had reinvigorated a team that was seventh in January. He'd scored seven in 14 games, and when he played, Milan invariably won.

There was also continental success for Milan in 2006/07. Having started in the qualifying rounds of the Champions League way back in early August, they faced Liverpool in the final in Athens on 23 May. It gave the Italian side a chance of revenge after the heartbreaking defeat in Istanbul two years earlier when they squandered a 3-0 half-time lead.

Ronaldo, sadly, missed the showpiece event, cup-tied after appearing in the group stage for Real Madrid. The grandest prize in European football continued to elude him and he would end his career as one of the greatest players never to have won the trophy. He celebrated on the pitch but looked uncomfortable; happy for his colleagues but knowing he played no role in the success. He seemingly didn't want to touch the trophy; it would be the closest he'd ever get to the holy grail of European football. 'I live football with a passion that doesn't give me any peace for not winning the Champions League – it's a trophy everyone would love to win,' he later said. 'It must have been torturous for him to be involved in the squad but unable to play in the Champions League-winning team,' said Emmet Gates. 'To be in and around the team but not having an actual role must have been tough. And the sad part was he only started one game for Madrid in the Champions League that season, but it was enough to cup tie him.'

* * *

The misfiring Borriello and Oliveira moved on to pastures new, while legendary defender Alessandro Costacurta retired. Ancelotti's most noteworthy pieces of business were the acquisitions of two Brazilians: midfielder Emerson from Real Madrid, and exciting youngster Alexandre Pato from Internacional for €24m. However, due to his tender age Pato – whose childhood hero was Ronaldo – was unable to play competitive games for the first half of the Italian season.

Ronaldo was hoping that his form in the second half of the previous campaign would continue but – as was the story many times during his career – injury scuppered his aspirations, preventing him from taking part in the entire pre-season programme. He missed out on yet more European silverware as in his absence Milan lifted the UEFA Super Cup with a 3-1 win over Sevilla in Monaco. He returned for an away victory at Cagliari in November, but then a calf injury ruled him out as the *Rossoneri* won the FIFA Club World Cup in Japan in December.

Following the winter break, Milan beat Napoli 5-2 at the San Siro with Ronaldo twice on the scoresheet. The infectious smile was back, and the forward could have been forgiven for thinking he was ready for another strong finish to a season. It was also the first and only time the much anticipated 'Ka-Pa-Ro' all-Brazilian forward line of Kaká, debutant and teenage sensation Pato, and Ronaldo, featured together for Milan. They scored four of the five goals and promised much. 'I'm happy about the compliments I have received but there was just one sensation on the pitch, and it was Ronaldo,' said a surprisingly modest and level-headed Pato after the game. Ancelotti was also impressed by the 31-year-old, 'Ronnie was something else. He's only been training for ten days. He showed great ability despite not being at his best.'

However, the two goals against Napoli would be his only ones of the season and his last in the European game. In mid-February, Livorno visited San Siro in Serie A and the European champions were eighth in the table, trailing their rampant cross-city rivals by 18 points. The enthusiasm felt ahead of the season had dissipated. And now they were losing 1-0 at home to Livorno. Looking for a creative spark, Ancelotti summoned Ronaldo from the bench, withdrawing Serginho after an hour. Shortly after entering the field, Ronaldo challenged for a header with Livorno's Portuguese midfielder José Vidigal. As he came down from the air his left leg gave way upon contact with the turf, and he fell to the ground in agony. Immediately sensing the gravity of the situation, the referee called for the medical team, and concerned players swarmed around the stricken star. Ronaldo was stretchered from the pitch, his hands covering his face. The referee awarded a penalty which Pirlo despatched to salvage a draw.

Having suffered the same injury twice in his right knee while playing for Inter, Ronaldo had now ruptured his left kneecap while playing for Milan. Clarence Seedorf accompanied his team-mate to the hospital. 'My heart stopped beating because it was like watching a repeat of the injury he suffered playing for Inter against Lazio,' said the Dutch midfielder, who was Ronaldo's Inter colleague at the time and on the pitch that day in the Stadio Olimpico in April 2000. 'His reaction was the same. Nobody wants to watch moments like that.' Seedorf's prognosis wasn't particularly positive, 'It's the third time it has happened to him. That's why I'm thinking it may be the end. We'll see what happens over the next six months – he now needs to focus on rehabilitation.' Other Milan figures responded to questions about Ronaldo's future. 'He fears for his career,' owner Silvio Berlusconi told Italian national broadcaster RAI. 'I called him last evening and told him to believe in himself. He has enormous physical potential. As a 31-year-old, he's very young. He has an extraordinary physique and I think within a few months he could return to being the champion that we all know him as.'

'He is still feeling a little pain, but it seems the tendon of the knee is in better shape than that of the right knee which was operated on eight years ago,' said Adriano Galliani. 'I am not a doctor and therefore I will not be making a guess at how long he will be out. He will need to stay in hospital about a week but after that I do not know where he will decide to go – whether he will return to Milan or go to Madrid with his son.'

'We're all very sorry and worried about what happened,' said Ancelotti. 'I don't want to say it's the end of his career because only time can decide – all we can do is stand by him.' Milan's medical officer Jean-Pierre Meersseman suggested that Ronaldo could make a comeback, but 'only if he is ready to face a long and difficult rehabilitation at 31'. The forward was once again operated on by Professor Gérard Saillant in Paris.

While Ronaldo was recuperating, Milan's season disintegrated. They were dumped out of the Champions League by Arsenal at the last-16 stage and after winning just half of their remaining Serie A games post-Livorno, Ancelotti's men finished fifth in the table and missed out on qualification for Europe's flagship knockout tournament. It could have been so different. 'Had Ronaldo not suffered that injury against Livorno, Milan's 2007/08 would have been very different,' said Emmet Gates. 'They destroyed Napoli and "Ka-Pa-Ro", while it doesn't roll off the tongue quite as majestically as "Ma-Gi-Ca", they only played a couple of games together. A huge shame, as Pato could have done the running for Ronaldo and allowed him to focus on scoring.'

In the summer of 2008, Ronaldo's 18-month contract with Milan expired. He left having scored nine goals in 20 games. It was a spell that promised much, in flashes, but ultimately disappointed. His time in European football was over. Out of contract and recovering from a serious injury, it was time to go home.

Chapter 12

Light at the End of the Tunnel

THERE WAS still time for one last dance. Although his career in Europe was over, one more opportunity awaited back home; a path well-trodden by a long line of ageing South American stars. After the expiry of his Milan contract in 2008 Ronaldo began training with Flamengo in a bid to regain his fitness. The Rio-based club famously rejected the forward as a youngster, but it remained close to his heart.

For four months Ronaldo trained with the *Rubo-Negro*. However, when it seemed like he would make a dream move to the most popular club in Brazil, interest from São Paulo outfit Corinthians – returning to the top flight at the first time of asking after winning the second division – muddied the previously crystal-clear waters.

Corinthians president Andrés Sánchez dampened enthusiasm when he said the potential deal to sign Ronaldo was financially 'impossible' yet before long confirmation came that an agreement was close. 'The Board of Sport Club Corinthians Paulista are negotiating the signing of forward Ronaldo,' read a statement on the club's official website. 'All the details are being sorted out by the president, Andrés Sánchez, the director of football,

Mário Gobbi Filho, and the director of marketing, Luis Paulo Rosenberg … In the upcoming hours, the parties should finish the negotiation and set a date to unveil the player.'

Gobbi Filho added, 'This is a very big marketing movement. It involves companies. It is not so simple.' Rosenberg said, 'This is more a marketing agreement than a player signing. That is why I am taking part in this. It will be a very original and profitable business.' Agent Fabiano Farah, acting on Ronaldo's behalf, said, 'There is a verbal agreement. In two days, it will be translated into a contract so Ronaldo can be considered a Corinthians player as soon as possible. Corinthians are being led by very serious people and we are very happy about that.'

In December 2008 Ronaldo signed a 12-month deal – with the option of another year – officially marking his return to Brazilian football after 14 years on the other side of the Atlantic. As usual, the Brazilian press was less than measured in its response. *Lance!* called him a 'phenomenal traitor' and Flamengo fans burned t-shirts featuring his image. Flamengo president Marcio Braga admitted the club had yet to offer him a contract, saying that they were waiting for him to return to full fitness. For the second time in his career, Flamengo had let Ronaldo slip through their fingers. 'I was surprised by the news,' Braga said. 'It was a disappointment. He said he wanted to stay here, he was training here. Flamengo did not receive even one "thank you".'

Ronaldo responded that while he was a Flamengo fan, he simply went where there was an offer on the table, 'I was training with Flamengo for four months and didn't receive any offer. Corinthians made an offer that will let me continue my career. I am very happy. It will be a big challenge for me but I will take it because I'm sure everything is going to be all right. Corinthians believe in me and have a fantastic project for 2009. I have a lot of confidence in myself. I am proud of myself. This fight has not been easy at any stage, but I'm managing to get through it. I am still a professional footballer; I still like big challenges and I think the Corinthians one is excellent for me. It is a big motivation in my return to football.'

He also told TV show *Globo Esporte*, 'I had to make a decision because I love playing football. My life is football. Corinthians came out as a light at the end of the tunnel, as they trusted in me and my potential. The beginning will not be easy but it is a big chance for me to return in good form. The Corinthians group of supporters is huge and maybe the best-organised. I am sure they will demand a lot, but I always have this in my life. There is no way to escape.'

The move to Corinthians polarised the opinions of those with a passionate interest in Brazilian football. 'I found out through my friends,' remembers Téo Benjamin, author of *Outro Patamar* which analysed Flamengo's successful 2019 campaign. 'Everyone started calling me. They didn't even support Flamengo and they were pissed. It was very surprising; it was out of the blue. He'd spent the last five years saying his dream was to play for Flamengo, that he wanted to finish his career there.' However, Benjamin did acknowledge that the club may have been so confident Ronaldo would join them that it perhaps led to complacency.

'It wasn't a betrayal, for me,' said Fernando Duarte. 'Flamengo is a complicated club, and it wasn't well-run at the time. Some hardcore Flamengo fans felt betrayed. It was a disorganised club, riddled with debt. It's different now, they cleaned up their act and are one of the richest clubs in South America but at the time it couldn't have been more different. It was the best decision for him, and it was nice to see him play in Brazil.'

Celso Unzelte, author, sports journalist and Corinthians fan, didn't see the big deal. 'It's [the feeling of betrayal] very common in Brazil when a football player is identified with one club and decides to join another; it was a natural reaction of the Flamengo fans.' Unzelte, a commentator on ESPN channels, did admit he was shocked at the acquisition, 'I thought it was a joke because Ronaldo was an international star.' Roberto Lioi, who was beginning his journalism career with Rádio CBN in 2009 when Ronaldo returned, said the story 'fell like a bomb on the news'.

It had been a tough ten months for Ronaldo since yet another career-threatening injury suffered against Livorno in February 2008. In April there was an embarrassing incident when he went to a Rio motel with three prostitutes, who turned out to be transvestites. An altercation led to a humiliating trip to the local police station, with Ronaldo claiming one of the party had tried to extort money from him. For weeks the star was the butt of jokes in Brazil. In October, he openly talked of his weight gain, and a month later he admitted he didn't think he would return to the football field. Yet here he was, lacing on a pair of boots once again as a professional.

His Corinthians debut came on 4 March 2009 in the first round of the domestic cup, almost four months after he penned his deal. The Juscelino Kubitschek Stadium, named after the 21st president of Brazil, was the setting. Itumbiara Esporte Clube were the opponents and, despite their modest status, the Goías outfit fielded the likes of Denílson – once the most expensive footballers on the planet when he transferred between São Paulo and Real

Betis in 1998, and someone whom Ronaldo knew well – Cristiano Ávalos, Caíco and former Brazil international forward Túlio.

Despite starting the match on the bench, it was clear that Ronaldo was the star attraction. Fans, journalists, photographers and even opposition players jostled to be close to him. With Corinthians two goals to the good, through Chicão and André Santos, Ronaldo entered the fray 22 minutes into the second half. The score remained the same and his side progressed to the second round of the cup. Leaving the field, Ronaldo was accidentally, but painfully, hit by a press microphone on the way back to the changing room.

Although he was past his peak as a player, the level of celebrity of Ronaldo remained high. 'Wherever Corinthians went, everyone wanted to see Ronaldo,' said Roberto Lioi. 'There was always a full stadium. After his debut, he barely managed to leave the field after the game. There was an invasion of journalists and fans who surrounded him. I was never able to do an exclusive interview with Ronaldo, but I participated in several press conferences and post-match interviews. What always surprised me is that everyone wanted to talk to Ronaldo. If another player had scored three goals and given victory to Corinthians, it didn't matter. We always wanted to talk to Ronaldo. And he was always very helpful. Even with all the media and fans all over him, he always had a lot of patience to answer questions. He did not shy away from the most sensitive topics. Even when some questions were inappropriate. They almost always asked about his weight. He responded on the field.'

In the following match, on Sunday, 8 March, Corinthians faced Palmeiras in the 12th round of the São Paulo State Championship. Diego Souza gave Palmeiras the lead in the third minute. Ronaldo came off the bench once again and fired a warning shot at Bruno Cardoso's goal, crashing a right-footed drive off the crossbar from outside the box. Then, in the second minute of injury time, Ronaldo headed in an in-swinging corner at the far post. The delirium of the crowd was palpable. Belying his advancing age, and well-publicised knee and weight problems, Ronaldo athletically hurdled the advertising hoardings behind the goal, scaling the fence that separated the pitch from the supporters. Part of the fencing gave way, and police rushed to the scene. No one was hurt, although Ronaldo was booked for his over-zealous celebrations. 'I'm very sorry for the incident, but I couldn't contain my emotions,' he said in a touchline interview immediately after the game. 'It was a big fright, it was a rather irresponsible attitude because the fence wasn't so strong after all,' he reflected at a later news conference. 'But you don't think at the time, you just want to celebrate with the fans.' It was obvious that the goal, and the reaction from rabid Corinthians fans, lifted a weight from Ronaldo's shoulders.

The point against Palmeiras left Corinthians three points behind their opponents, who led the table, although the main consideration was finishing in the top four to qualify for the play-offs. Corinthians were well-placed to do just that. In the following round, at home to São Caetano, Ronaldo once again proved decisive, bagging the winner in the 50th minute on his full debut. On a rainy night in the Pacaembu, with the score 1-1, Ronaldo swept in a low Dentinho cross with his right foot after it had been cleverly dummied. He was replaced by Escudero after 78 minutes, leaving the field to loud cheers from the 31,700 spectators present. Even though there was still time to play, the game might as well have been over because of the euphoria in the stadium.

On 25 March Corinthians hosted Ponte Preta in the state championship. The visitors took the lead before Ronaldo equalised with a nonchalant penalty, and for his second goal he showed quick feet in the box to control the ball before deceiving the defender and finishing. The visitors grabbed a late leveller. Six days later Corinthians beat Ituano 3-0 at home. Ronaldo scored one of his side's goals with an easy finish from 12 yards.

Corinthians finished third in the group to progress to the final four where they faced São Paulo over two legs. After winning 2-1 at home, Corinthians went to the Morumbi where a 2-0 victory sealed their passage to the final. Ronaldo scored the second in the 57th minute, winning a foot race with the defender before clipping the ball over the goalkeeper from 20 yards. 'The supposedly "chubby" Ronaldo reached 36kph and won several races against the younger opponents of São Paulo,' recalled Lioi.

Corinthians took on Santos in the state championship final and were already 1-0 up when Ronaldo scored after 25 minutes. The veteran controlled a high ball over the defence before drilling it home with his left foot. Santos pulled one back but then came a moment of genius even a peak Ronaldo would have been proud of. After 77 minutes he sprung the offside trap, chopped inside from the right and then chipped the goalkeeper to give his side a commanding 3-1 lead. 'No one could have scored the goal he scored,' said Lioi. 'At the beginning of 2009, Ronaldo looked like the phenomenon that made history with the Brazilian national team, Barcelona, Inter and Real Madrid.'

The goal impressed a certain Santos legend, watching from the stands in the Vila Belmiro, a place where he'd wowed crowds decades before. 'It was a goal worthy of Pelé,' *O Rei* himself said modestly. Ronaldo was equally pleased with himself. 'Each goal I score, I lose a kilo,' he told reporters. Celso Unzelte called it a 'historic goal'. The second leg produced a 1-1 draw, meaning Corinthians were state champions, undefeated in 23 games. The first trophy of the Ronaldo era was in the cabinet.

When Ronaldo signed, some suggested it was a publicity stunt, but even the most sceptical were being won over. One club director suggested his comeback was a story worthy of a Hollywood film. Brazil's president, affectionately known as Lula – who served between 2003 and 2010, and took office for another spell in January 2023 – even chipped in, suggesting an international recall should be considered. 'I think that if he came back to the national side, it would be extraordinary,' said Lula. 'I admire people who never give up.' Many agreed with Lula. A poll ran by TV Globo suggested 70 per cent believed Ronaldo deserved another chance with the *Seleção*.

Corinthians continued to progress in the Copa do Brasil. Misto-MS were beaten 2-0 in the second round then, in the first leg of the third round, Corinthians lost 3-2 against Club Athletico Paranaense. However, a week later they overturned the deficit with a Ronaldo brace. His first came in the 55th minute when he received the ball with his back to goal, held off the defender, then turned and shot across the goalkeeper from the edge of the box and into the far corner. Thirteen minutes later another cocky penalty sealed their passage to the last eight. Ronaldo almost walked up to the ball, feinted, and waited for his adversary to move before rolling it into the empty area of the net. It was the penalty of a confident man.

Fluminense and Vasco da Gama were eliminated in the quarter- and semi-finals respectively. Then, on 17 June,

Corinthians beat Internacional 2-0 in the first leg of the final. Ronaldo got the second in the 53rd minute. Cutting inside the defender, Ronaldo finished at the goalkeeper's near post with his left foot. The roar from the crowd was deafening and the smile on the striker's face as his team-mates rushed to congratulate him was priceless. The second leg finished 2-2, a result which handed Corinthians the cup. It was Ronaldo's second piece of silverware in just a little over three months since his debut. It came with a bonus: a spot in the 2010 Copa Libertadores.

Corinthians finished tenth in Brazil's Série A – which ran from May to December 2009. Ronaldo missed much of the 38-game campaign due to injury, scoring a respectable 12 goals in 20 matches. Flamengo, aggrieved at losing out to Ronaldo, repatriated Adriano from Italy, and he was instrumental as they won the championship.

* * *

In February 2010 Ronaldo signed a contract until the end of the following year, suggesting he would retire upon its expiry. 'I have renewed for another two years and they will be the last of my career. I have already decided that,' he said.

The Copa Libertadores, a trophy that Corinthians had yet to win, was now the focus. As well as success in South America's flagship club tournament, the resurgent Ronaldo had one eye on the upcoming World Cup in South Africa. 'It's a thing that can still happen to me,' he said, referring to a potential call-up by manager Dunga, his old international team-mate. 'I am determined. I want to give my best, have fun and I hope to finish by winning the Libertadores.' The group proved easy enough, with Corinthians notching an impressive 16 points in six unbeaten games. Ronaldo scored important goals in two wins over Paraguayan outfit Cerro Porteño.

Then came a powder-keg clash with Flamengo in the last 16. The Rio outfit won the first leg 1-0 in the Maracanã. On home turf, on 5 May, Corinthians led 1-0 in the second leg before Ronaldo made it 2-0 on 39 minutes with a diving header. He waved his arms at the crowd as if to request further noise to get them over the line. However, Vágner Love pulled one back for Flamengo and sent them through on away goals.

In the 2010 state championship, Ronaldo failed to score as Corinthians finished fifth, failing to progress to the play-off stage. Santos's Neymar, a rising star and Ronaldo's heir as the national team's attacking lynchpin, was declared the tournament's best player.

The Série A campaign began well enough. Just four days after the disappointing Copa Libertadores exit, Ronaldo scored an 84th-minute winner against Club Athletico Paranaense. His next goal came three months later, after a prolonged absence through injury, a penalty in a 1-1 draw against the same opposition, in a 45-minute cameo. Mano Menezes, Ronaldo's manager since he returned to Brazil, left Corinthians in July to replace Dunga at the helm of the national team following their quarter-final exit in South Africa.

Following another spell on the sidelines, Ronaldo returned against Guarani on 17 October. In stifling 33°C heat he played 90 minutes and had two goals disallowed in the goalless draw. It left Corinthians without a win in seven. Ten days later he scored in a 1-1 draw away to Flamengo. The following week he bagged a late brace in a 4-0 thumping of Avaí, one of which came from the penalty spot; he scored another penalty in a 1-0 win over former club Cruzeiro. Ronaldo's return to form and fitness reinvigorated Corinthians – as did the sacking of Menezes's replacement, Adilson Batista, who lasted less than three months – and the club ultimately finished third, just three points behind eventual champions Fluminense. Had Ronaldo been fit for the entire campaign, who knows what might have happened. And had Tite – the new manager and the man who later led the national team between 2016 and 20122 – been in charge for the whole campaign, who knows. Although a spot in the Copa Libertadores had been earned, 2010 – the club's centenary – was a bit deflating following the two trophies won the previous year.

* * *

In 2011 the Copa Libertadores was once again the focal point for Corinthians – who remained the only big club in São Paulo state yet to have won it – and Ronaldo. Timão were Brazil's fifth-seeded team and therefore had to overcome a two-legged qualifier against modest Colombians Deportes Tolima to reach the group stage. At the Pacaembu, the first clash ended goalless. A week later Corinthians travelled to Colombia's mountainous centre, where two goals in eight second-half minutes sent Tite's men out of the prestigious competition. It was a scandal. Never had a Brazilian club exited the competition at such an early stage. The fact that the opponents had no pedigree at the highest level only exacerbated the backlash. Being the highest profile of Corinthians' roster, Ronaldo was the target of much of the anger.

Graffiti and banners were found at the club's training ground. One read 'O Gordo'. Former Corinthians star Neto, now a pundit on Brazilian TV, accused Ronaldo of playing solely for money. Upon their return to Brazil, Corinthians players were met at the training ground by several hundred angry fans who threw stones at the bus, hurled obscenities, and damaged cars. Roberto Carlos, citing concerns over his safety following the incident, requested to leave. According to Celso Unzelte, he'd received much more criticism than other stars because he hadn't travelled to play in Colombia. His contract was cancelled by mutual consent and he headed to Russia.

Ronaldo defended himself on Twitter, admitting his role in the defeat in Colombia but condemning the violence. It was enough to make him think about retirement. 'I considered [stopping], talked to my family and some friends and made the decision to continue because it is a difficult time, but I'm sure we will turn around once again to reverse this sad situation we are living,' he said in an exclusive interview with TV Globo. 'I will continue and fulfil my contract with dignity and honour the Corinthians shirt until the end of the year.'

Despite the defiant promise to continue, Ronaldo changed his mind, the Tolima debacle proving to be the final straw. On Monday, 14 February 2011 he headed to Corinthians' training ground one last time. Wearing a Nike polo shirt, and accompanied by two of his four children, sons Ronald and Alex, an emotional Ronaldo interrupted a training session at 10.30am. After five minutes of discussion and hugs he left the field to a standing ovation, something he'd become accustomed to throughout his career.

At 12.40pm, he was scheduled to tell the media. In true Brazilian style, Ronaldo kept them waiting until just after 1pm. 'As you can imagine and you heard during the whole weekend, I'm here today to [confirm that] I'm closing my career as a professional player,' he said, tearfully. 'I thanked all the players, the coach

Tite, for all the minutes, for every second I was with them. It was a very beautiful career, wonderful and exciting. [There were] a lot of defeats and a lot of victories. I made a lot of friends, and I can't recall any enemies. I'm ending my career due to some very important reasons.'

The 34-year-old continued his 45-minute speech, 'Everyone knows about my injury history. I have had, in recent years, a sequence of injuries that go from side to side, from one leg to the other, from one muscle to the other. These pains made me anticipate the end of my career. Also, four years ago I found out when I was at Milan that I suffered from hypothyroidism. It is a disorder that slows down the metabolism and, in order to control it, it is necessary to take some hormones that are prohibited in football, because they can be accused of doping. I imagine many must be sorry for making fun of my weight, but I don't hold a grudge against anyone.'

Such was his emotion, he had to pause numerous times to take deep breaths and wipe away tears. To distract himself, he was on Twitter and gave attention to his sons sitting beside him. 'I have many thanks to make,' he continued. 'To all the clubs I've been to: São Cristóvão, Cruzeiro, PSV, Barcelona, Inter Milan, Real Madrid, Milan … I will thank Corinthians very soon. I want to thank all the players who played with me and those who played against, those who were loyal and those who were also disloyal. Thank the coaches I had a good relationship with and the ones I had disagreements with. And also to thank the sponsors who always believed in me.'

Corinthians were given a special mention, 'I have to thank all the Brazilians who cried with me when I cried and who fell with me when I fell. But, from this entire Brazilian crowd, I want to thank Corinthians. I've never seen a crowd so vibrant, so passionate and so dedicated to their football team. It is true that sometimes this demand for results makes it aggressive and out of control. But I couldn't imagine living without Corinthians. I thank Andrés, who is my brother, and I say that I will continue to be connected to the club in whatever way he wants. You will often find me cheering for Corinthians at the stadium. I take this opportunity and publicly apologise for the failure in Libertadores' path.' He announced that, after hanging up his boots he would focus on charity and business interests.

Writing in the Players' Tribune in 2015 and looking back at his decision to retire, Ronaldo said, 'I knew I had to stop. If I couldn't be the player that I wanted to be on the pitch, if I couldn't have the same feeling, then I couldn't be out there at all … I lived my dreams. How many people can say that about their lives? To have seen and lived in so much colour.'

The comeback kid, who had defied the odds many times throughout his career, had run out of steam. And while his Corinthians adventure didn't provide a fairytale ending, his presence at the club was transformative. He joined as the *Timão* were emerging from the dark depths of the second division, scoring 35 goals in 69 appearances. They may not have won the Brasileirão or the Copa Libertadores but his signing was a success. 'It was a very good surprise,' said Celso Unzelte, who compared Ronaldo to other icons who have represented the club such as Rivellino, Sócrates and Garrincha. 'I expected little, but he gave more than just publicity. He won two very important competitions and was the big Corinthians star in 2010, the club's centenary year. He was a veteran, overweight, and still better than all others in the field.'

* * *

'Nobody imagined that the club could sign Ronaldo,' said Roberto Lioi. 'Ronaldo's arrival at Corinthians is a milestone for the club. From 2009 onwards, the club only grew. With the help of Ronaldo and the various sponsorships he brought, Corinthians built a new training centre and had money to make signings. Like everything else in Ronaldo's life, he generates a lot of impact wherever he goes. And once again Ronaldo was a game-changer. He helped the club on the field and did a spectacular job of rebuilding an almost bankrupt club.'

Like a pebble in a pond, the ripples from Ronaldo's acquisition continued after he left. In 2012 Corinthians landed the Copa Libertadores, going on to beat Chelsea to win the FIFA Club World Cup. 'Corinthians were even world champions in 2012 and one of the causes, for sure, was the change of route that the club had with the arrival of Ronaldo,' said Lioi.

When one door closes, another opens. Boots firmly hung up, it was time to break out the briefcase. Ronaldo was set to embark on his new life as a businessman.

Chapter 13

Life Goes On

EVEN DURING the latter days of his playing career, Ronaldo was strategically thinking about his next move. A 400-capacity nightclub spread over three floors in upscale Rio neighbourhood Leblon, a physiotherapy clinic, motorsport team, marketing agency, talent agency, and the R9 Family Office – which provides property and financial management for high-performance athletes – were just a handful of projects he invested in after retiring. The varied portfolio yielded mixed results; some became defunct while others were continuing to thrive at the time of publication.

Ronaldo also missed football, but not enough to want to coach. As an industry it's too volatile, too stressful, and offers little long-term security. Coaches are too often one poor result or an owner tantrum from losing their job. Instead he wanted a role that would give him control. He sought to be the man in charge. The decision-maker, not the person decisions were made about.

His first attempt at football club ownership was a baptism of fire. In December 2014 it was announced the Brazilian had invested in Fort Lauderdale Strikers of the North American Soccer League (NASL), nominally the second tier in a country without a true football pyramid. Ronaldo had spent six months discussing his potential role before his shareholding – thought to be in the region of ten per cent – was confirmed. Never one to dream small, Ronaldo announced some bold plans for the historic franchise that, in a previous lifetime, boasted the likes of George Best and Gerd Müller. 'I could not be happier to be part of both the Strikers, a team with an extraordinary legacy, and the NASL, with its rich history and tremendous growth potential,' he said. 'I am confident that my experience, vision, and work will be instrumental in helping to elevate the Strikers, the NASL, and soccer in the US to the highest level. South Florida, where there are so many soccer fans, is the ideal place for my Strikers.' He mentioned the possibility of a new stadium, the launch of soccer schools around Florida, and a potential move to MLS. At around the same time, a familiar face also joined the NASL: his former Real Madrid team-mate Raúl signed for New York Cosmos.

Ronaldo met with MLS commissioner Don Garber in New York City. 'I told him, "We want to join MLS, but we don't have the $100m,"' the Brazilian said, referring to the franchise fee required to enter the league. 'I said, "It's better that you [adopt] promotion and relegation to improve football in America." And he said, "That's not working here." He was glad to hear from me, but at the end he just said, "If you want to join us, pay the franchise fee." After that meeting, I started looking for new opportunities.' A spokesperson for MLS denied Garber said this.

Less than two years after acquiring a stake in the Florida club, things began to turn sour. On 1 September 2016 the principal owner, fellow Brazilian Paulo Cesso, announced he would no longer be funding the team. The NASL, losing clubs to MLS and other organisations in the confusing soccer landscape of the

United States, and seeing dwindling attendances, ceased to exist altogether just a couple of years later.

* * *

The star's first foray into the boardroom may have ended in defeat, but no doubt valuable lessons were learned. As he did as a player, Ronaldo responded to the setback, showing the famous mental resilience that helped him recover from serious injuries. The 42-year-old – who spent time living in London, studying sports management and marketing – was busy plotting his next move. On 3 September 2018 he was unveiled as the new majority owner of Spanish club Real Valladolid. For €30m – approximately one-tenth of his net worth by conservative estimates – Ronaldo acquired a 51 per cent stake. He would grow his shareholding over time and is now thought to own approximately 80 per cent of the club's shares.

At a press conference, Ronaldo outlined his plans for the club, 'We want to grow and reach where our will allows us. I will use four words to define our politics: competitiveness, transparency, revolution and social. I assure you that you will find me as a lover of Castilla-Leon, Valladolid and Real Valladolid.'

Ronaldo's predecessor stated that the decision to sell his majority stake and welcome the Brazilian into the club was not just a financial decision. 'It was not an economic issue, but now Valladolid can play in other leagues, Ronaldo puts us on the map now,' began Carlos Suárez. 'I thought it was the best for the club, and that's what I bet, you'll see that it's the ideal option for Valladolid.' Alongside Suárez, Ronaldo met city mayor Oscar Puente at Valladolid's town hall, where they had lunch. 'He is a sports world icon and the operation seems interesting,' Puente told *AS*. 'Along with Michael Jordan, he is the only person who has a lifetime contract with Nike. It would bring a lot of value to Valladolid.'

'We want to build the best team possible to compete and will be transparent in our management,' said Ronaldo. 'Trust us to consolidate Real Valladolid in La Liga and for us to be able to grow the enthusiasm that there is. Together, I'm convinced that it will be very difficult to beat us. I want everyone to help build this club and I invite the fans to take part in this project. Give us ideas, opinions, criticisms and hopes. I want you to be a part of the present and future of Real Valladolid.'

Many questioned what had attracted Ronaldo to the modest club in the first place. The location is favourable, just a two-hour drive from the Spanish capital, where he retained a home. There was his passion for football, without subjecting himself to the volatile world of coaching. 'I love it,' Ronaldo told Grant Wahl in a 2021 interview with *Sports Illustrated*. 'I was my whole life loving football … It's what I want to do and what I know how to do. And that was why I bought a team.'

The deal also represented value for money. The modest club, without a major honour to its name, had spent most of its existence oscillating between Spain's top two tiers. 'I looked a lot, in the [English] Championship but everything was too expensive,' said Ronaldo. 'The Premier League is a complete success worldwide and so is the Championship. But you had to have £60m, so I then looked in Portugal and Spain, where the prices were more affordable … When I was no longer thinking about that, I heard there was an opportunity at Valladolid.'

Ronaldo saw a lot of potential. Although not one of the largest, the Estadio José Zorrilla – constructed for the 1982

World Cup – was packed most weeks with loyal fans. Like any businessman, a return on investment was on his mind, but leaving a legacy on the club and city was also important to him. He stated he would be a serious and conservative owner, and a hands-on one, albeit without interfering. 'Do you think I'm going to buy the club then go on holiday the next day?' he said to journalists when asked how committed he would be. Ronaldo opted to work from an office in Madrid, typically spending two days a week in Valladolid.

A humble Ronaldo worked hard to learn his new trade, immersing himself in every facet and level of the club. The new regime cleared debts and earmarked a chunk of cash to improve the stadium and training ground. To win hearts and minds, an email address was publicised, and fans were encouraged to communicate their questions, suggestions and concerns, with a promise of a reply within 48 hours. Knowing that competing with the likes of Real Madrid and Barcelona was all but a pipe dream, Ronaldo was determined to invest in the youth team and blood youngsters, an antidote to paying soaring transfer fees.

After four years in the second tier, Real Valladolid were back in the big time for the 2018/19 season after gaining promotion via the play-offs. However, when the transfer window closed – days before Ronaldo's unveiling – they had spent just €3m, less than 18 of the other 19 top-flight clubs. Manager Sergio González, who took the reins in April 2018, had a tough task on his hands.

When the *Blanquivioletas* lost Ronaldo's first game, 1-0 at home to Alavés, they had yet to score a league goal in four attempts. Real Valladolid ultimately finished four points above the drop zone having scored just 32 times in 38 matches, the worst record in La Liga that season. In his heyday, Ronaldo would have scored that amount on his own. The stresses of his first season as an owner, and the highs and lows of the relegation battle, took their toll, forcing Ronaldo to visit a doctor at the end of the campaign due to high blood pressure. Although it may never replace the exhilaration of playing and scoring goals on the biggest stage, the tension of running a club is altogether different and anxiety-inducing.

Ten days after the season had finished the club, and Spanish football, was rocked by Operation Oikos. At 8am on 28 May 2019, Valladolid favourite Borja Fernández – who had announced his retirement and was expected to take up a non-playing role within the club and was due to meet Ronaldo that day to discuss it – was arrested. The former Real Madrid man was taken away in handcuffs and spent three days in a cell, although he denied any wrongdoing. The 2-0 defeat to Valencia on the final day of the season – which gained *Los Che* qualification to the Champions League – was under scrutiny, particularly the nature of the errors which led to both goals. The investigation would rumble on for years to come and, eventually, Borja's name was cleared.

* * *

In the summer of 2019 Ronaldo treated the team to a trip to Ibiza, then in pre-season they went to California, the first time the club had toured outside of Europe. It showed the global reach that came with Ronaldo's presence, which opened new markets and increased the attraction of the project to players and investors alike. They faced San Jose Earthquakes in a friendly; four days later they lost on penalties to Cardiff City in Edmonton, Canada. Season tickets were selling faster than ever, with 21,600 snapped up ahead of the campaign. The stadium had received plenty of work over the summer and was looking excellent in resplendent purple.

At the halfway stage of the season Valladolid had won just four league games. And in January 2020 a new primary sponsor was announced: Estrella Galicia. The beer brand had previously been involved with the club but would now adorn the first-team shirts, an agreement worth five times more than the previous sponsor was paying. 'The Rivera family [owners of Estrella Galicia] is an example for us of how to evolve without losing the essence, and I believe that our two entities are in a very similar moment of sustainable growth,' said Ronaldo. 'From the first contact, we had an instant identification, since we share the same philosophy of constant search for excellence. Estrella Galicia has a history of success in sports sponsorship and I am convinced that we will grow together. It will be a cycle of victories.'

La Pucela lost 1-0 at home to Real Madrid, then two days later they made a signing that was supposed to be a big statement of intent. Former French international Hatem Ben Arfa, who had won honours with the biggest clubs in his homeland as well as representing Newcastle United, penned a six-month deal. The 32-year-old was keen to sign the contract with Ronaldo – a childhood hero of his – by his side. Although Ben Arfa was dubbed 'Ronaldo's first *galáctico*' he flopped, making just five appearances before departing.

With Ben Arfa omitted from the squad, Valladolid beat Espanyol 2-1 on 23 February in a crucial relegation clash. Their opponents had spent €40m in January alone, and the winning goal came from Sergi Guardiola. The forward was the subject of much interest the previous summer but Ronaldo's veto had kept him at the club. It was looking like a wise decision. In late

February, Ronaldo travelled to the Sport Summit Mexico, where he did an on-stage talk with La Liga president Javier Tebas, the two discussing the Valladolid project among other topics.

On 8 March 2020, Valladolid were drubbed 4-1 at home by Athletic Bilbao. Then, what no one saw coming: a global pandemic. The spread of the COVID-19 virus forced a halt to football worldwide, with Spanish football's governing body, the Liga Nacional de Fútbol Profesional, officially suspending the season on 23 March. Ronaldo's girlfriend, Celina Locks, was in Brazil; he was stuck in his Madrid flat on his own.

On 1 May, after almost two months of isolation, the players were allowed outside to exercise. Training resumed, albeit with restrictions. Everyone was tested, and the players were split into small groups. During the pandemic every employee was paid in full; nobody was made redundant. Ronaldo was showing his caring, generous side. The remaining 11 fixtures were to be played behind closed doors, squeezed into a punishing 36-day schedule.

Valladolid recommenced their campaign on 13 June with a 2-1 victory in another crucial relegation battle away to Léganes. After what was described as '11 finals' Valladolid stayed up, finishing in 13th place, six points above the drop zone. It was an undoubted success. At just €35m, coach Sergio González had the second-lowest budget in La Liga to play with, a figure dwarfed by the approximately €600m at the disposal of Ronaldo's former clubs, Barcelona and Real Madrid.

* * *

The 2020/21 season proved much tougher for Valladolid. On 6 March they beat Getafe 2-1 at home, only their fifth win in 26 league games. It would be their last. 'I'm not going to stay here forever, because I have other things for the future in my mind,' said Ronaldo, in quotes carried by *Sports Illustrated*. 'But it's too early to talk about that. I want to make this club much better and bigger than when I got it. After that, let's see. For now, it's just: keep working and keep the club in the first division.' Valladolid failed to win any of their last 12 games and were relegated with just 31 points, having scored a paltry 34 goals in 38 matches. Fans were unhappy with Ronaldo for being absent from the stadium on the day that relegation was confirmed, and the first cracks started to show in the relationship. Less than 24 hours after Valladolid lost to champions Atlético Madrid on the final day of the season, manager González – and sporting director Miguel Ángel Gómez – were fired. In April 2021 it had been revealed that 84 per cent of the club's revenue came from TV, an income that would plummet following relegation.

* * *

The new manager for the 2021/22 season was Pacheta, who had taken Huesca down to the Segunda División alongside Valladolid. In October 2021 Ronaldo told *FourFourTwo* that he was 'extremely happy with how things are going around here'. By the winter break, thanks to the goals of Israeli striker Shon Weissman, the club's record signing, Valladolid were in the play-off spots and in with a shout of promotion at the first time of asking.

When Ronaldo initially purchased the Spanish club, he said his original idea was to 'expand the business and try to build a network of teams', perhaps in the mould of Red Bull or the City Football Group. In December 2021 he did just that, buying a controlling stake in Cruzeiro, where he started his professional journey as a player.

This was made possible in August 2021, when Brazil's Congress passed a law allowing football clubs to become businesses. Historically, Brazilian clubs were typically structured as not-for-profit member associations. The fans were the members, and they elected the presidents. Clubs were closed off to investors but were somewhat protected from the boom-and-bust cyclical nature of capitalism. However, the system does come with its issues. As with any election, there is always the risk of someone under-qualified attaining the position, and their ego taking control. Football becomes more about politics, and the personalities involved than it does about the sport. Crucially, especially as South America fell behind Europe with every passing transfer window, these people were unable to plough funds directly into the club, leaving them at a disadvantage in a globalised world.

Taking advantage of the new law, Cruzeiro were the first club to switch from a non-profit entity to a corporate one. Effectively, the football operation was split from the social club and was allowed to attract investment. The social club side of the club was still run by members who elected their leaders. In November 2021 the limited company was formed and on 17 December the members voted to allow a 90 per cent stake in the company to be sold. 'Among the great challenges ahead of us, one of the biggest was to make Cruzeiro a club-company,' said chairman Sérgio Santos Rodrigues. 'It was a long job, from the first day of the administration, with dozens of meetings many of them in the Senate and the Chamber of Deputies.'

Ronaldo completed the purchase through his company Tara Sports, pledging to invest R$400m (approximately £50m) in the coming years. The deal was done with the assistance of Brazilian investment bank XP, who said in a statement, 'It seeks to help the

Brazilian football industry with professionalisation, capitalisation and opening new opportunities.' CEO José Berenguer said, 'This is the first bit of business in a relevant new front for the investment banking market in Brazil, the country of football … I have no doubt this is transformational in the history of Brazilian sport. We will have clubs that are stronger, with the capacity for global investment. Brazilian football will never be the same again.'

Ronaldo's bid fended off interest from Fenway Sports Group, the owners of Liverpool as well as American sports teams Boston Red Sox and Pittsburgh Penguins. 'I am so happy to have concluded this operation,' he said, adding he wanted to 'give back to Cruzeiro and take them where they deserve to be.' Preaching caution, he continued, 'We have a lot of hard work to do. There's nothing to celebrate yet but we bring a lot of hard work and the ambition to make Cruzeiro great again.' On Instagram, he wrote, 'It's my turn to try and open doors for the team. Not as a hero. Not with superpowers to single-handedly change reality. But with immense responsibility. With intelligent and sustainable management for medium- and long-term growth.' Pelé tweeted, 'Congratulations and good luck on this new journey, my friend.'

The Cruzeiro Ronaldo was buying had been spiralling out of control for almost a decade. The club won the league in 2013 by a landslide of 11 points, with the highest average attendance in the division. In 2014 they were once again the best-supported team, and the margin was ten points as they lifted the title. The Copa do Brasil in 2017 and 2018 added further silverware to the bulging cabinet. Then, inexplicably, the Foxes were relegated in 2019 for the first time in their history, having previously belonged to a select group – including São Paulo, Flamengo and Santos – of Brazilian clubs that had never played outside the top level.

On 26 May 2019, TV Globo aired an exclusive revealing there was a police investigation into the club's financial dealings with suspicions of money laundering, document forgery, and other law-breaking practices as well as breaches of both CBF and FIFA rules. To ease the club's debts, the team of Wagner Antônio Pires de Sá – elected Cruzeiro president in 2017 – effectively handed over a chunk of some of the player's economic rights to creditors, even though this practice was outlawed by FIFA four years earlier. A transfer ban placed on the club only exacerbated their already deteriorating position.

In 2020 Cruzeiro finished 11th in Série B, earning the unwanted accolade of being the first big club to have been relegated and not bounced back immediately. The following year they finished 14th, just five points ahead of the demotion spots to the third tier. Ronaldo's timely intervention came less than a month after the end of this disastrous campaign. With debts of almost R$1bn, Ronaldo's investment came with the club closer to the threat of extinction than it was to a return to the top flight.

* * *

Entering the final day of the 2021/22 season, Valladolid were in third place in the Segunda División, on 78 points; Almería and Eibar occupied the automatic promotion spots with 80. At half-time it was goalless at the Estadio José Zorrilla against Huesca, a result which would have confined Valladolid to the play-offs. Yet three second-half goals for Ronaldo's men changed the complexion of the promotion race. Both of their opponents dropped points, and Valladolid snuck into the top two at the crucial moment. It was only the fifth time they'd been second all season, and it was when it mattered; they were heading back to Spain's top flight.

Following promotion, Ronaldo made good on a promise to complete an arduous 280km journey between Valladolid's stadium and the pilgrimage site in Santiago de Compostela. Coming full circle, the city was the sight of one of his greatest moments as a player, the wonder goal against SD Compostela in October 1996. The 46-year-old documented the journey on social media. 'I promised that if we came back [to La Liga], I would do the Camino de Santiago,' said Ronaldo. 'I will do it by bike as I can't run … It will be beautiful. I know that I will suffer physically but it will be an unforgettable experience.'

* * *

In April 2022, as the Spanish season was heading towards its exciting climax, the Brazilian league was just getting started. Days after Ronaldo's regime had taken over Cruzeiro, Vanderlei Luxemburgo exited. Luxemburgo had worked with Ronaldo during his playing days, with Brazil and later Real Madrid. They won the 1999 Copa América together for the national team. It was Luxemburgo's third spell managing Cruzeiro and the decision was based primarily on finances. 'To adjust the accounts to the club's economic reality, the board was instructed not to continue with the existing coaching staff,' an official statement read.

On Monday, 3 January, Luxemburgo's replacement was unveiled: 38-year-old Paulo Pezzolano. During his playing days the Uruguayan had spent most of his career in his homeland, except for short spells in Brazil, Spain, China and Mexico. He began his coaching journey in 2017, with two jobs in Uruguay preceding a role in Mexico with Pachuca. While playing for

Athletico Paranaense, in 2006, Pezzolano met Paulo André, who later worked with both Cruzeiro and Real Valladolid. 'I am very excited to participate in this Cruzeiro project,' said Pezzolano at his unveiling. 'We are going to need you ... I know the strength of the fans. Now, more than ever, we will be together.' Pezzolano fitted the bill of what the club was looking for: a coach with youth, hunger, and one who would work within the new, responsible, financial reality.

On 21 September, Cruzeiro welcomed Vasco da Gama to the Mineirão for what was their 106th consecutive match in the second tier. Before the game, the home fans displayed a Ronaldo-themed *tifo*, depicting their owner as a youngster in his playing days for the club. Cruzeiro won 3-0, the result – as well as defeats for Grêmio and Bahia – cementing their promotion back to the top flight with seven games to spare, a Série B record. It came just 94 days after Ronaldo's other club, Real Valladolid, achieved their promotion to La Liga. 'This is just the icing on the cake,' said Ronaldo, who celebrated on the pitch after the match. 'We've worked hard to deserve this. That night was very special. Congratulate the players, coaching staff, my management team, but especially the fans who suffered for almost three years. Today is the day of glory. Thank you, I want to thank them for their support. Now let's celebrate for a few days and start thinking about next year.'

On Instagram, Ronaldo wrote, 'Life has no script, but what a movie plot! In December last year, when I announced my intention to [take control of] Cruzeiro, the certainty I had was a lot of hard work ahead. Four months after starting the club's reconstruction project, we signed a contract and made the purchase official. Five more months to go and the best birthday present I could get: we're back in Série A! Football is not just a game. The fastest [promotion] in Série B history was not defined in a single match. And let's go for more, much more! Let's go together!'

The final table showed the champions finishing 13 points clear, scoring the most goals and boasting the meanest defence. At one point they went on an eight-match winning streak. The arrival of Ronaldo had proven transformative. 'In addition to the initial amount invested that helped the club to pay several short-term debts, Ronaldo implemented a radical change in the club,' said Roberto Lioi. 'He cut higher wages, removed people who were doing nothing and turned Cruzeiro back into a professional club. In 2023 Cruzeiro is already fighting on an equal footing with other great teams. It was a great move by Cruzeiro to sell football shares to Ronaldo.'

* * *

With both teams back in the top flight, Ronaldo could have been forgiven for thinking this ownership lark was easy. Or at least becoming easier, as he learned tough lessons along the way. However the 2022/23 Spanish season brought him back down to earth with a bump. After a 6-0 drubbing at the Bernabéu in April, a game in which Karim Benzema scored a seven-minute hat-trick as Valladolid's defence capitulated, Pacheta was dismissed with *La Pucela* 16th in the table. In a statement, the club said that, '[We] recognise the important trajectory of the coach and the role that he has carried out with the club since his arrival, but, with the only aim of remaining in the highest division at the end of the season, this decision has been taken.' The departing Pacheta, unhappy with his compensation package, initiated legal proceedings against his former club. His case had not been resolved at the time of publication.

His replacement was a familiar face. Paulo Pezzolano had left his Cruzeiro role a couple of weeks earlier after losing the semi-final of the Mineiro state championship. 'Honestly, I wasn't 100 per cent,' he told reporters. 'A club as big as Cruzeiro needs a coach who is at 1,000 per cent.' In a subsequent social media post, Pezzolano added, 'I promise the fans that if I manage elsewhere this year, it's not going to be in Brazil. I couldn't trade Cruzeiro for another club. That would be a lack of respect toward the fans.' He was true to his word, rocking up in Spain shortly after. Seven points from the first three games was a promising start but then followed five consecutive defeats. A five-point haul from the final three games wasn't enough, and Valladolid went down in 18th place.

Pezzolano's replacement at Cruzeiro was Pepa, continuing the trend of Portuguese managers in the Brazilian league. The 42-year-old signed a contract until the end of the year, an indictment of the short-term nature of modern football. After injury curtailed his playing career, he started coaching at a young age and after working in his homeland, he joined Cruzeiro from a club in Saudi Arabia.

At the time of writing Real Valladolid were gearing up for another season in the Segunda División, whereas Cruzeiro sat comfortably in mid-table of Brazil's top flight, a position that if maintained would give them continental football in 2024.

With two clubs, and once suggesting he wanted a global empire along the lines of the Red Bull or City Football Group, perhaps we will one day see Ronaldo adding a third club to his portfolio. Like his playing career, Ronaldo is learning that in business nothing comes easy, that it is full of ups and downs. Time will tell what he can achieve in the boardroom, but if he shows similar grit and determination that he showed to rise to the top of his profession and return to the highest level on the pitch against all the odds, he will achieve his goals with Real Valladolid, Cruzeiro, and perhaps other clubs.

Chapter 14

Legacy of a Phenomenon

AN EXCEPTIONAL, unusual, or abnormal person, thing, or event; a prodigy. That's how the *Penguin English Dictionary* defines the word 'phenomenon'. Even that doesn't quite capture the brilliance of Ronaldo, especially in this era of hyperbole in which we are currently living.

Ironically, he didn't like the nickname at first, due to the pressure and expectation of people thinking he was flawless. In recent years he's been referred to as the other Ronaldo. The original. The Brazilian. Sometimes in less favourable terms, referring to his weight, something he was sensitive about later in his career. The current generation may hear the name Ronaldo and think of Cristiano, yet before the fleet-footed teenager joined Manchester United from Sporting Lisbon in 2003 his Brazilian namesake had already been the most exciting footballer on the planet. He'd risen, fallen, risen again, and even scored a hat-trick at Old Trafford – before many present that night had even heard of the Portuguese – leaving the pitch to a standing ovation from the entire stadium. Manchester United fans used to sing 'There's only one Ronaldo' which was tongue-in-cheek, more designed to support Cristiano than denigrate the Brazilian.

Although his right foot was stronger, he scored many, and great, goals with his left. Inside and outside the box. Poachers' goals. He could use brute force and pace when he needed to; finesse, accuracy, skill and deftness when that was required. In the eyes of many, he's the greatest centre-forward in the history of the game. However he wasn't like an old-fashioned striker. Yes, he led the line and played centrally. But he made excellent runs, varied his position and could dribble like the best and trickiest wingers out there. He was perhaps the first modern forward, the type that would go on to be comfortable and interchangeable across a front three. At his peak he was the complete player. He was also two separate players. During the early part of his career, pre-1999, he was a destructive force of nature. From 2002 onwards, he was less mobile and more of a goal scorer.

Ronaldo's goalscoring résumé speaks for itself. By the time of the World Cup in 1998 he had scored 180 senior professional goals – in 200 appearances. He was just 21 years old. This was an era before Lionel Messi and Cristiano Ronaldo ripped up the rule book, scoring one or more per game on average. Generally, in the 1990s and prior, a top striker would be happy with one every two games. Not Ronaldo, he was built differently. His goals came in Brazil, the Netherlands, and Spain's La Liga. Then in 1997 he went to the toughest league in the world, one renowned for defensive genius: Italy's Serie A. He didn't care, didn't respect reputations, and the goals flowed.

He won the World Cup twice, and numerous other tournaments with Brazil. He won the Intercontinental Cup, La Liga, the UEFA Cup, the Cup Winners' Cup, domestic cup competitions in the Netherlands, Spain and Brazil, the Supercopa de España twice and the São Paulo state championship. Individual awards were repeatedly bestowed upon him. Being named in teams of the year or teams of the tournament, or finishing as the top scorer, almost became mundane. His trophy cabinet for personal gongs alone would outstrip most clubs. He was most notably the FIFA World Player of the Year on three occasions; in 2003 the culmination of his remarkable redemption arc was rewarded with the Laureus World Comeback of the Year award.

Ronaldo has been involved with charity work throughout his career, including serving as a goodwill ambassador for the United Nations. He has played in numerous charity matches to raise money for good causes across the globe and is the founder of the Phenomena Foundation which helps communities in his native Brazil. As a young man, Ronaldo undertook compassionate trips – although ones that made his advisers shudder – to war-torn Kosovo, and Foligno, in Italy, following an earthquake. He went to the notorious San Vittore prison in Milan to visit the inmates.

Despite his fame reaching its peak in the era before social media, he now has tens of millions of followers across various platforms. In 2004 the *Washington Post* claimed he was the third most recognisable person in the world, only behind the Pope and the incumbent United States president George W. Bush. 'Ronaldo is one of the few Brazilians who can go anywhere in Brazil and be recognised by everyone,' said broadcaster Roberto Lioi. 'Even those people who don't like football.' Through what he's earned with his various clubs as well as deals with global corporations, Ronaldo has stacked enough money to last several lifetimes, a lot of it with Alexandre Martins and Reinaldo Pitta, whom he worked with until 2004. His highest-profile collaborator is Nike, whose Oregon headquarters now features a large bronze statue of the Brazilian overlooking a football field.

When looking at someone's legacy it's important not just to focus on numbers, but also the intangibles. What trails they've blazed, what imprint they left on those with whom they crossed paths. Ronaldo has touched many hearts. This is certainly true of his first 11-a-side football team, São Cristóvão de Futebol e Regatas. 'The identity of the whole club pretty much revolves around him,' said Thiago Vancellote, the club's director of commerce and marketing between February 2019 and November 2021. 'The name of the youth category is nicknamed the "Fenômeno Factory", the trophy room has a lot of trophies that he won.' The stadium is even named in Ronaldo's honour, and a large sign reading 'The Phenomenon was born here' adorns the building behind one of the goals. During the 2014 World Cup in Brazil, the ground became something of a cult tourist attraction, with fans from all over wanting a glimpse of the place where Ronaldo took his first steps in the 11-a-side game.

He is fondly remembered as a player by Cruzeiro fans of a certain vintage and has even returned to a club for the only time in his career, to take an ownership role. Although PSV Eindhoven was a stepping stone to grander stages, it got his foot in the European door and led him to bigger and better things. 'I'd seen him on television at PSV and thought "wow",' said Luis Enrique, Ronaldo's colleague at Barcelona during that explosive 1996/97 season, in an interview with *FourFourTwo*. 'He's the most spectacular player I've ever seen. He did things I'd never seen before. We're now used to seeing Messi dribble past six players, but not then. He was strong, a beast – but a kid, as well. He was typically Brazilian, doing the samba in the dressing room. Him and Giovanni would make music with a wastepaper bin.

They danced. I love that atmosphere, the group feeling that Brazilians have.'

French defender Laurent Blanc – who also spent one year in the Catalan capital – told *El País*, 'I've never seen any other player score an impossible goal in every match he plays. You think back to Maradona's brilliant goals in Mexico [in the 1986 World Cup], but with Ronaldo, it happens every day. An extraordinary goal now and again, that's one thing. But this guy does it week in, week out.'

Óscar García Junyent, a local lad who lived the dream of playing for Barcelona, had the extra joy of playing with Ronaldo. 'Until that moment, I'd never seen anyone play football with such technical ability, creativity and precision at that incredible speed,' he told Bleacher Report. 'What stood out to me, and all of us, from the moment we met Ronnie was that he could do things which other players found very difficult and make them look easy. But he could also produce those things while running at an unbelievable, explosive pace.

'Back then, he was all fibre and muscle. It's incredible that his body could change as much as it has from then until he stopped playing. He was a perfect physical specimen. Such incredible power matched to his technical skills could make him unstoppable.

'Not only was he correctly praised for playing with a smile on his face, for making it look like he was having fun, he was also a guy who seemed perpetually in a good mood, always joking around the training ground.

'One of our permanent jokes all that season was me demanding he slow down when he was celebrating a goal. He was so much faster than me that I had to ask him to put the brakes on when he did his famous arms-out celebration just so that I could catch up with him and get in the goal photo. I'd shout, "Brakes, pal, brakes on!"

'I've worked around Barcelona while Leo Messi's been there and at his best. I've never seen anything like [Ronaldo]. For all that we saw in matches from Ronaldo when he was at the Camp Nou, we all witnessed him do simply astounding things with the ball in training … Just remarkable stuff. The pressure was off, and Ronnie had the ability to do anything. Nobody could stop him in training.

'And if you took just that single year at Barcelona, you'd have said that he was guaranteed to go on and be at least one of the top four or five players in the history of the game. That's because his nickname was accurate. It was an epic season, and he was a football phenomenon.'

South African defender Quinton Fortune also shared his memories of Ronaldo with Bleacher Report, 'I've heard stories about Michelangelo's statue of David, although I've never visited Florence to witness it, but I imagine it must look like Ronaldo did back then … He was physical perfection, and he seemed like a mythical figure. I love [Lionel] Messi, I played many times with Cristiano [Ronaldo] and I adore him, Neymar is outstanding, Ronaldinho was exceptional – but if you put all of them together, you might get what Ronaldo was that season … Some players were technical, some were quick, some were strong, some were smart. Ronaldo was all of those. He was a beast; it was unfair to everyone else … It was great to be part of that season [Fortune was an Atlético Madrid player in 1996/97] because I witnessed beauty. Poetry, painting, all the arts. This was their equal. I just appreciate to this day that I shared a pitch with him.'

Ronaldo's manager during his sole season at the Camp Nou also spoke positively about him. 'That was the best season he's had in his whole career,' said Bobby Robson. 'He was scintillating on the pitch, and injury-free … I've been in soccer a long time and I don't think I've ever seen a player at 20 have so much … When he stripped, he looked like a boxer. He had wonderful biceps and shoulders with terrific definition. He was so strong and so quick.' Robson's assistant, a young Portuguese translator-turned-coach, gave high praise. 'After Maradona the best player was Ronaldo,' said José Mourinho. 'It is my opinion that he is the best of the last 20 years.'

Although La Liga was strong in the mid-to-late 1990s, it wasn't what it would go on to become when Messi, Ronaldo, Guardiola and Mourinho were dominant. In 1997 Serie A was the place to be. The best, highest-paid stars graced Italian football meaning it was a perfect fit for a man of Ronaldo's talents. 'Ronaldo was probably one of the best team-mates I ever had as a player,' said Argentine midfielder Diego Simeone. 'I'm pretty sure I enjoyed Ronaldo at his best. He was strong, healthy, without all those knee problems he had to endure afterwards. And at his tender age, that made him a completely extraordinary player.'

'I learned more from Ronaldo than he did from me that season,' said Luigi Simoni, Inter manager in 1997/98. 'He always was in a positive mood. He was a model for everybody in and outside the pitch.' Simoni's successor, Romanian Mircea Lucescu, said, 'Ronaldo is the greatest player I have ever coached.' Inter president Massimo Moratti said, 'Ronaldo was the most powerful centre-forward in history. It was an honour to have him at Inter at the pinnacle of his career.'

In 2018 Inter's Hall of Fame was created to recognise the legacy of some of the greatest to have worn the famous black and blue shirt. Ronaldo, who scored 59 goals in 99 games for the *Nerazzurri*, was included in the first raft of inductees alongside Javier Zanetti, Lothar Matthäus and Walter Zenga. 'If you asked any Inter fan to name their greatest XI, they would pick players who were long serving or won numerous trophies,' explained Richard Hall, Inter's English-language content provider. 'They'd begrudgingly put Ronaldo up front because he was just that good. Every other player in that XI would have almost died for the club and he's the one they couldn't omit.'

Paolo Maldini and Alessandro Nesta, two of the greatest Italian defenders of the modern era, rate him highly. 'I've never seen a player with his speed and power,' said AC Milan legend Maldini, who ranks Ronaldo up there with Maradona in terms of his Serie A opponents. 'It was the worst experience of my career,' said Nesta, referring to the 1998 UEFA Cup Final in which Ronaldo's Inter destroyed his Lazio side. 'Ronaldo was simply unstoppable.' Marcel Desailly of Milan and France said, 'I've never seen a player able to show such precise control at such high speed. Watching him was like watching a character in a video game.'

After several injury ravaged years at the San Siro, Ronaldo 2.0 pitched up at Real Madrid. A different player but still brilliant. 'When he was through on goal you might as well go and hug him then because you know it's in,' said Bernabéu legend Fernando Hierro. 'He had a stratospheric vision, he thought so fast.' Steve McManaman struck up an unlikely friendship with the Brazilian following his move to the Bernabéu. The Liverpudlian and Ronaldo shared a similar sense of humour and a laid-back demeanour, and McManaman helped him learn English using lyrics from American rap songs. 'You don't know the geezer, but you know he's a nice bloke,' said McManaman. 'He's infectious.'

Jorge Valdano, the Argentine who has a long-standing relationship with Real Madrid, once famously described Ronaldo as 'not a man, he's a herd'. Valdano also said, 'Ronaldo finishes chances with surgical precision and in the build-up to chances he always takes the right option of where to be and when to sprint.' Despite the fact they spent little time on the pitch together, and he was ostensibly signed from Manchester United in 2006 to be Ronaldo's replacement, Ruud van Nistelrooy is full of admiration. 'The best player I ever played with was at Real Madrid,' said the Dutchman. 'Ronaldo *Fenomeno*, Brazil … Fantastic player. What special skills he had and especially the kind of guy he is too so, for me, the best ever.' In 2013, Marca.com asked its readers to compile their best-ever all-foreign Real Madrid XI. Ronaldo made the cut, partnering Cristiano Ronaldo and Alfredo Di Stéfano in a dream attack.

After falling foul of Capello, Ronaldo returned to the San Siro, this time in the red and black. A *Derby della Madonnina* goal against Inter made him the only man in the history of the game to have scored for both Milan clubs in the derby, as well as Barcelona and Real Madrid in *El Clásico*.

Towards the end of his spell with Milan, Ronaldo was embroiled in an extortion scandal with three prostitutes in a motel room when he was recovering from an injury back in Brazil. 'That type of event would have finished the career of 99 per cent of footballers,' said journalist and Real Madrid fan Eduardo Álvarez. 'No one even remembers that anymore. Right after the scandal he appeared on *Globo*, the top-rated audience show which happens on Sunday night, and spoke for 20 minutes, not even mentioning the event but saying he made a mistake. Then the whole thing disappeared. This could have finished anyone but Ronaldo.

People like him so much that nothing negative gets attached to him. It's impressive.' After his Milan contract expired he joined Corinthians, when many expected him to sign for boyhood club Flamengo. It was the last club of his career.

On 7 June 2011, Brazil faced Romania in a friendly in São Paulo. Ronaldo came on in the 30th minute, playing until half-time. There was a small ceremony to mark his farewell appearance. 'Thanks to all of you for what you did in my career,' an emotional Ronaldo said, wearing his iconic number nine and speaking into two microphones attached to a podium. 'When I cried, you cried with me. When I smiled, you smiled with me. See you soon, but on the sidelines this time. I'm very proud of being Brazilian.'

Thanks to his performance at the 2002 World Cup, he became only the third footballer after Eusébio and Pelé to be named the BBC Overseas Sports Personality of the Year. His former international coach Mário Zagallo once said, 'Ronaldo has so much natural ability ... Ronaldo's speed on the ball, balance and dribbling are incredible. Yes, he can rewrite the record books.' When he scored against Ghana in 2006, he did just that, becoming the leading scorer in World Cup history.

And for most people, the greatest legacy they'll ever leave behind is their children. Ronaldo had four, all born between 2000 and 2010. His sons, Ronald and Alexander, came first; daughters Maria Sophia and Maria Alice followed. He had a vasectomy after Alexander's birth but has revealed he has sperm on ice in case he wants a fifth child. He is currently engaged to Celina Locks, who will become his fourth wife if they tie the knot. Although he lives in Madrid, he regularly visits Brazil to see his children and to look after his business interests there.

It is often said Ronaldo's career could have been so much more if it weren't for the serious, debilitating injuries he suffered. 'I still think about where I would be if those knee injuries hadn't happened,' Ronaldo wrote in the Players' Tribune. 'If it wasn't for injury, I think he would be talked about on the same level as Pelé and Maradona,' said goalkeeping icon Gianluigi Buffon. 'He had all the skills needed to be the best ever. He was like an alien because of what he could do on the pitch.'

'Had he managed to stay free of injury, he had every chance of becoming the best footballer ever,' said Bobby Robson. 'He marked an entire era, a player above millions of others, and yet he could have marked that era even more if he had not had injuries,' lamented Fernando Hierro.

Despite his achievements, Ronaldo did only win one domestic title (La Liga in 2002/03 with Real Madrid) and failed to grasp that elusive Champions League trophy. When Milan won it in 2007, he was cup-tied. He came close with Real Madrid in 2003. In 2019, *FourFourTwo* named him the best player never to win the competition, and Sky Sports put him behind Maradona as the greatest not to win the Champions League or European Cup. Football history has taught us that creating a winning team is more complex than just amassing a certain number of talented players and expecting results. Players' personalities and how individuals work together are just as important as individual brilliance. Success isn't guaranteed. And that's what makes us love football: the uncertainty. The endless circle of hope, despair, and hope again. It's Ronaldo's career to a tee.

Timing is important and perhaps Ronaldo was at the right clubs, just at the wrong time. It's fantastical but imagine him in the PSV team that won the European Cup a few years before his arrival, alongside Romário who joined the club the summer of the 1988 triumph. Imagine him in Cruyff's Dream Team or playing alongside Messi under Pep Guardiola at the Camp Nou. Iconic sides that came before and after his season in Catalonia. Imagine him playing alongside his namesake Cristiano Ronaldo as Real Madrid won four Champions Leagues in five years. Imagine if he'd stayed fit at Inter and been around when they won their treble in 2010, under a man he knew well, José Mourinho. Imagine if he hadn't been cup-tied when at Milan in 2007. If there is such thing as a footballing higher power, perhaps they struck him down with injuries to level the playing field, to give everyone a chance of competing during his era. Imagine the havoc he would have wreaked on defences had he been fortunate enough to enjoy an injury-free career. What if, what if, what if.

Ronaldo might not have had the incessant longevity of many a modern footballer, but perhaps that is part of his charm. Had he not had a lifetime aversion to training, had he not loved parties, women, beer and junk food, his career may have lasted longer. But would he be the same man, would he be so popular, would he have played with a smile on his face; would his career have intrigued me enough to write a book about him?

Part of his alluring charm is the smile, the carefree approach to the game, as if he were still kicking a ball about on the streets of Bento Ribeiro or the golden sands of Rio's stunning beaches. Footballers are human, they aren't robots. They are fallible; they have bad luck. The human element of the game is what makes us fall in love with football and hate it in equal measure at times. Ronaldo had fun on and off the pitch, but make no mistake he was a winner. He was the archetypal flawed genius. And we love him for it. He is simply phenomenal.

Bibliography

Books:

Agnew, P., *Forza Italia: The Fall and Rise of Italian Football* (London: Ebury Press, 2007)

Ball, P., *White Storm: 100 Years of Real Madrid* (Edinburgh: Mainstream Sport, 2002)

Bellos, A., *Futebol: The Brazilian Way of Life* (London: Bloomsbury Publishing, 2002)

Burns, J., *Barça: A People's Passion* (London: Bloomsbury, 1998)

Campomar, A., *Golazo: A History of Latin American Football* (London: Quercus, 2014)

Clarkson, W., *Ronaldo! King of the World: The True Story of the World's Greatest Footballer* (London: Blake Publishing, 2002)

Cox, M., *Zonal Marking: The Making of Modern European Football* (London: Harper Collins, 2019)

Duarte, F., *Shocking Brazil: Six Games that Shook the World Cup* (Edinburgh: Arena Sport, 2014)

Ferdinand, R., *Rio: My Story* (London: Headline, 2006)

Ferguson, A., *Managing My Life: My Autobiography* (London: Hodder & Stoughton, 1999)

Foot, J., *Calcio: A History of Italian Football* (London: Harper Perennial, 2007)

Goldblatt, D., *Futebol Nation: A Footballing History of Brazil* (London: Penguin, 2014)

Maradona, D., *El Diego* (London: Yellow Jersey Press, 2005, trans. Marcela Mora y Araujo)

McManaman, S. & Edworthy, S., *El Macca: Four Years with Real Madrid* (London: Pocket Books, 2005)

Mosley, J., *Ronaldo: The Journey of a Genius* (Edinburgh: Mainstream Publishing, 2005)

Robson, B., *Farewell but Not Goodbye: My Autobiography* (London: Hodder & Stoughton, 2005)

Stam, J., *Head to Head* (London: Collins Willow, 2001)

Venables, T., *Born to Manage: The Autobiography* (London: Simon & Schuster, 2014)

Websites:

90min.com

Bbc.co.uk/sport

Bleacherreport.com

Cbc.ca

Chinadaily.com.cn

Cruzeiro.com.br

Edition.cnn.com

Elpais.com

Eurosport.com

Eurosport.co.uk

Espn.co.uk

Fcbarcelona.com

Fenomenos.org

Fifa.com

Fourfourtwo.com

Gentlemanultra.com

Ge.globo.com

Givemesport.com

Goal.com

Guinnessworldrecords.com

Hojeemdia.com.br

Hopkinsmedicine.org

Independent.co.uk

Inter.it/en

Irishtimes.com

Latimes.com

Managingmadrid.com

Marca.com

Mirror.co.uk

Nike.com

Planetfootball.com

Realmadrid.com

Rsssf.org

Si.com

Skysports.com

Smh.com.au

Sproutwired.com

Terra.com.br/esportes/

Theguardian.com

Theplayerstribune.com

Uefa.com

Washingtonpost.com

Newspapers and magazines:

FourFourTwo

Mundial

World Soccer